Cornish in Michigan

DISCOVERING THE PEOPLES OF MICHIGAN
Arthur W. Helweg, Russell M. Magnaghi, and Linwood H. Cousins, Series Editors

Ethnicity in Michigan: Issues and People
Jack Glazier and Arthur W. Helweg

French Canadians in Michigan
John P. DuLong

African Americans in Michigan
Lewis Walker, Benjamin C. Wilson,
and Linwood H. Cousins

Albanians in Michigan
Frances Trix

Jews in Michigan
Judith Levin Cantor

Amish in Michigan
Gertrude Enders Huntington

Italians in Michigan
Russell M. Magnaghi

Germans in Michigan
Jeremy W. Kilar

Poles in Michigan
Dennis Badaczewski

Dutch in Michigan
Larry ten Harmsel

Asian Indians in Michigan
Arthur W. Helweg

Latinos in Michigan
David A. Badillo

South Slavs in Michigan
Daniel Cetinich

Hungarians in Michigan
Éva V. Huseby-Darvas

Mexicans and Mexican Americans in Michigan
Rudolph Valier Alvarado
and Sonya Yvette Alvarado

Scots in Michigan
Alan T. Forrester

Greeks in Michigan
Stavros K. Frangos

Chaldeans in Michigan
Mary C. Sengstock

Latvians in Michigan
Silvija D. Meija

Arab Americans in Michigan
Rosina J. Hassoun

Irish in Michigan
Seamus P. Metress and Eileen K. Metress

Scandinavians in Michigan
Jeffrey W. Hancks

Cornish in Michigan
Russell M. Magnaghi

Discovering the Peoples of Michigan is a series of publications examining the state's rich multicultural heritage. The series makes available an interesting, affordable, and varied collection of books that enables students and lay readers to explore Michigan's ethnic dynamics. A knowledge of the state's rapidly changing multicultural history has far-reaching implications for human relations, education, public policy, and planning. We believe that Discovering the Peoples of Michigan will enhance understanding of the unique contributions that diverse and often unrecognized communities have made to Michigan's history and culture.

Cornish in Michigan

Russell M. Magnaghi

Michigan State University Press

East Lansing

∞ The paper used in this publication meets the minimum requirements
of ANSI/NISO Z39.48-1992 (R 1997) (Permanence of Paper).

Michigan State University Press
East Lansing, Michigan 48823-5245

Printed and bound in the United States of America.

13 12 11 10 09 08 07   1 2 3 4 5 6 7 8 9 10

LIBRARY OF CONGRESS CATALOGING-IN-PUBLICATION DATA
Magnaghi, Russell M.
Cornish in Michigan / Russell M. Magnaghi.
p. cm. — (Discovering the peoples of Michigan)
Includes bibliographical references and index.
ISBN 978-0-87013-787-7 (pbk. : alk. paper)
1. Cornish Americans—Michigan—History. 2. Cornish Americans—Michigan—Social life and
customs. 3. Cornish Americans—Michigan—Social conditions. 4. Immigrants—Michigan—History. 5. Michigan—Ethnic relations. 6. Michigan—Social life and customs. 7. Michigan—Social
conditions. I. Title.
F575.C6M34 2007
977.4'0049167—dc22
2007023830

Discovering the Peoples of Michigan. The editors wish to thank
the Kellogg Foundation for their generous support.

Cover design by Ariana Grabec-Dingman
Book design by Sharp Des!gns, Lansing, Michigan
Cover photo: A typical Cornish picnic, Copper Country, Michigan (Courtesy Tom Friggens).

Michigan State University Press is a member of the Green Press Initiative and is com-
mitted to developing and encouraging ecologically responsible publishing practices.
For more information about the Green Press Initiative and the use of recycled paper
in book publishing, please visit *www.greenpressinitiative.org*.

Visit Michigan State University Press on the World Wide Web at *www.msupress.msu.edu*

To Cornish-Americans Doris Bable; Tom Friggens;
Merton, Milton, and Sidney Holman; and Scott Holman,
whose support was essential to this study.

BOOK ACKNOWLEDGMENTS

You would not be reading this monograph without the active support of series editor Arthur Helweg. Not only did he include the Cornish experience in his vision for this series, but he also invited me to author the work.

Although the story of the Cornish immigrants in Michigan has been told many times, this study took on a new perspective. I introduced a new focus on the story, one that involves Cornish immigration not only to the Upper Peninsula but to the Lower Peninsula as well. As a result I used a variety of institutional sources and would like to acknowledge and thank the staffs of the Longyear Research Library of the Marquette County History Museum; the State Library of Michigan; the Burton Collection of the Detroit Public Library; the archives of Michigan Technological University; the University of Michigan's Bentley Library; the library of Michigan State University; and the Lilly Library of Indiana University. Jack Deo of Superior View Studio allowed me to research his photographic collection.

There were also numerous individuals who provided me with important personal experiences and insights and in particular photographs. Ray Leverton was a key figure, providing me with names and stories that got the project started. The Holman brothers—Merton, Milton, and Sidney—spend a long afternoon with me, telling of their family experiences. The same was true of Doris Bable and the late Gertrude Gruber in the Lower Peninsula. Scott L. Holman of Bay City shared family records with me. Norm Gruber was helpful in sharing materials from Cornwall, and Tom Friggens located photographs of his grandfather from the Copper Country. Then Secretary of State Candice Miller took time from her busy schedule to locate photographs as well. Sarah Bottrell, Arlene Pearce Felt, Betty Leverton, and Merton Holman generously shared their traditional recipes.

I thank all of these people and many others who assisted me. I hope that the finished work meets expectations and readers enjoy the new insights provided into the Cornish experience in Michigan.

SERIES ACKNOWLEDGMENTS

Discovering the Peoples of Michigan is a series of publications that resulted from the cooperation and effort of many individuals. The people recognized here are not a complete representation, for the list of contributors is too numerous to mention. However, credit must be given to Jeffrey Bonevich, who worked tirelessly with me on contacting people as well as researching and organizing material.

The initial idea for this project came from Mary Erwin, but I must thank Fred Bohm, director of the Michigan State University Press, for seeing the need for this project, for giving it his strong support, and for making publication possible. Also, the tireless efforts of Keith Widder and Elizabeth Demers, senior editors at Michigan State University Press, were vital in bringing DPOM to fruition.

Otto Feinstein and Germaine Strobel of the Michigan Ethnic Heritage Studies Center patiently and willingly provided names for contributors and constantly gave this project their tireless support. Yvonne Lockwood of the Michigan State University Museum has also suggested and advised contributors.

Many of the maps in the series were prepared by Gregory Anderson at the Geographical Information Center (GIS) at Western Michigan University under the directorship of David Dickason. Additional maps have been contributed by Ellen White.

Other authors and organizations provided comments on other aspects of the work. There are many people that were interviewed by the various authors who will remain anonymous. However, they have enabled the story of their group to be told. Unfortunately, their names are not available, but we are grateful for their cooperation.

Most of all, this work is a tribute to the writers who patiently gave their time to write and share their research findings. Their contributions are noted and appreciated. To them goes most of the gratitude.

ARTHUR W. HELWEG, *Series Co-editor*

Contents

Introduction

everal ethnic groups have come to Michigan from the British Isles— Cornish, English, Irish, Scottish, Welsh—each of which can be studied indi-
vidually because of its significant role in American history. The record
shows that some of the early nineteenth-century Cornish immigrants were
farmers who settled in the Lower Peninsula. However, since most of the early
Cornish immigrants were miners, much of their influence was in the Upper
Peninsula and thus much of this story will concentrate on the northern portion of Michigan. It was in this region that many of the underground miners
from Cornwall got their start before they migrated to other mining regions
throughout the United States, bringing with them their expertise. The Cornish people have been shaping and influencing Michigan for over a century
and a half.

Cornwall and the Cornish People

Who are the Cornish? In the early Stone Age there were few people in Cornwall. Around 4000 B.C., a group of settlers migrated from Europe over a drift
across a land bridge, bringing to the area the first stone tools. The remains
of a Stone Age settlement have been found at Carn Brea near Redruth. The

name "Cornwall" comes from *Coronovii,* meaning hill dweller, and *Waeles,* meaning strangers.

About 2500 B.C., a trade began in tin and copper, whereby traders brought bronze tools and gold ornaments, which were exchanged for these metals. These people were well organized, living in villages and practicing farming and metalworking. The remains of Bronze Age Cornish villages can still be seen on Bodmin Moor and the West Oenwith Uplands.

Around 1000 B.C. a group of Celtic warriors arrived from Europe. They brought with them the knowledge of iron forging and were able to create weapons. These Celts were the ancestors of the modern Cornish. They were village dwellers who farmed; mined for tin, copper, and iron; and smelted and worked the metal. Most of their settlements were located on hilltops or on promontories that could easily be defended. Hence the word "Car" or Caer" in Cornish place names comes from the Celtic "ker," meaning fort, and "dinas," meaning hill.

The coming of the Romans to Britain in 55 B.C. had little influence on the Cornish. The Cornish geography kept the Romans at bay, while the Roman presence kept other raiders away. As a result the Cornish Celts were left to themselves. Christianity was brought to Cornwall in 520 A.D. by St. Petroc from Wales, who is considered the "official" patron saint of Cornwall. Earlier St. Piran, the patron of Cornish tinners, arrived in Cornwall. His influence can be seen in the internationally recognized flag of Cornwall, which is a white cross on a black field. Legend has it that liquid tin in the shape of a cross once appeared among the black ash after smelting, when St. Piran was present.

Through the Middle Ages mining continued to play an important role in Cornish life and its economy. Through the centuries the land between St. Ives and Perranporth was the Cornish mining center. At first tin was recovered from the beds of streams in a process called "streaming." This was practiced for more than two thousand years, until scarcity prompted the search for the metal-bearing strata underground. From that point forward, men worked hillside holes and progressed to digging shallow, vertical shafts.

Because of its isolated location, Cornwall was the last portion of English territory to come under Saxon influence. It was not until the Norman Conquest in 1066 that Cornwall began its integration into England. Cornwall was given to William the Conqueror's half brother, Robert, and Launceston was

St. Piran

St. Piran was a hermit, and he is considered the patron saint of the tin miners and tinners who live in Cornwall, near Padstow. He probably was born in Ireland and landed at the sandy beach of Perranporth. He is credited with bringing Christianity to England. In some lists St. Piran is referred to as Perran or Pyran.

St. Piran is alleged to have built the first oratory on Penhale Sands, which is considered the earliest Christian site in England and is an important component of Cornwall's cultural heritage. The original oratory was abandoned by the eleventh century, when encroaching sand dunes covered the site. A second church near the same location was also overwhelmed by sand; a third church dedicated to St. Piran, still exists in Perranzabuloe. During the medieval period, pilgrims visited the site of the church, which was also on the route taken by pilgrims sailing to the shrine of St. James in Compostela, Spain. The site of the church initially flourished and grew rich but suffered greatly during Tudor times, when its importance and wealth declined. Nevertheless, the church remained the center of the community.

St. Piran is known for having "rediscovered" tin mining. While St. Piran burned a fire on a black stone, tin in the stone melted and rose to the top to form a white cross. This event inspired the St. Piran Cross which today is the national flag of Cornwall. St. Piran's commemoration day is March 5.

made his headquarters. For the next few hundred years, Cornwall was ruled by a succession of relatives of the Norman and Plantagenet kings. In 1337 the first Duke of Cornwall was Edward the Black Prince, son of Edward III.

Beginning in the fifteenth century the Cornish began to play a noticeable role in English affairs. They joined the victorious Lancastrians in the Wars of the Roses (1455–85). Sir Humphrey Arundell led the "Prayer Book Rebellion" of 1549, in which the Crown imposed the Book of Common Prayer and ended various religious ceremonies. The Cornish rebels, who knew little English, had demanded the restoration of the Latin service. In response the Church of England and the state suppressed the "Revolting Cornish" at Exeter, where hundreds were killed and Cornwall was brought in line with Westminster.

Throughout these hundreds of years the Cornish in their isolated state dedicated their lives to fishing and mining. The wealth of Cornwall was beneath the earth in the form of tin and then copper. Hence the toast, "fish, tin, and copper" was appropriate. Richard Carew in his *Survey of Cornwall* published in 1602 provides a finely detailed description of the county.[1]

Scholars have noted that "no county in England has a stronger individuality than Cornwall, whether in economic or social conditions, in history, nomenclature, tradition, or even in the physical characteristics of the land." They are not a populous people, and their land of Cornwall is a mere 1,300 square miles that juts into the sea as the southwesternmost part of Britain. Physically Cornwall is a promontory measuring some seventy-five miles in length and forty-five miles at its widest point along the Devon border. The Tamar River forms a greater part of the boundary with Devon, and its valley divides the high moors of Devon and a succession of similar broad-topped hills that form the backbone of the Cornish promontory. A bare and desolate moorland extends along the high ground, and well-wooded valleys extend from the moorland to the sea on both sides. The estuaries are deep and provide access for ships. Except for the estuaries, the coast is rock-bound and the cliffs provide scenery unsurpassed in Britain. Given Cornwall's southern location, the climate is mild and allows flowers and vegetables to flourish and supply distant markets.

The Cornish in the Americas

Because of its location, Cornwall played a role in the exploration and early settlement of Anglo North America. In 1536, Robert Hore, who led an expedition to Newfoundland, took with him M. Weeke, a person with a Cornish name and described as "a gentleman of West country." He was possibly the first Cornishman to visit the New World. Between that time and 1587 various expeditions landed at Mounts Bay, Padstow Bay, and St. Ives on their return to England. The port of Plymouth on the Devon border with Cornwall saw Humphrey Gilbert sail for Newfoundland, Richard Grenville for Virginia, Martin Frobisher and John Davis for the Northwest Passage, and Sir Walter Raleigh for Guiana. The most successful of all of these adventurer-explorers, Sir Francis Drake, sailed from his hometown of Plymouth. The church of St. Budeaux was the site of Drake's marriage in 1569 and contains the tomb of Sir Fernando Gorges (d. 1647), the first governor of Maine. Bartholomew Gosnold sailed in 1602 from Falmouth, reached America, named Cape Cod, and sailed south to Virginia. Between 1689 and 1840, Falmouth was the chief Atlantic packet station in England. At first it served Corunna, Spain, and, after 1702, the West Indies. In a 1773 letter written by M. F. Rishton, he noted that the town of Tingmouth, Devon, was "the emporium of all the productions of Newfoundland and Labrador." He further elaborated that if Mrs. Rolp "wishes to have spermaceti candles of a beauty superior of any made in Europe I can procure her any Quantity."[2] From these pieces of evidence it can be assumed that many unknown Cornishmen participated in the voyages of exploration and commerce that sailed to the New World.[3] Given the location of Cornwall and neighboring Devon, it was natural that these regions played a continuing role in the development of colonial America.

The Cornish connection to the United States can be traced back to the colonial era, when Cornish colonists joined their English compatriots and sailed for the New World. In 1621 the Pilgrims left from Plymouth, and William Trevore sailed with them as a sailor-laborer. He remained in America for a year and then returned to England, where he told exaggerated stories of the land and its resources. Information like this caused Cornishment to migrate to Massachusetts, where the towns of Falmouth and Truro were named after Cornish towns. Historian Samuel Eliot Morison wrote that the town of Marblehead attracted fisherfolk from Cornwall and the Channel Islands. They maintained their distinct dialect and a typical jealous exclusiveness for over two hundred years. These Cornishmen were concerned more about fishing than religion, and the Puritan magistrates did not interfere with them as long as the community "made fish." This is summed up in a Marblehead fisherman's reproof to an exhorting preacher: "Our ancestors came not here for religion. Their main end was to catch fish." In 1650s Maryland the Cornish names of Bain and Vaughn appear in the records of the colonial assembly.

We do not know when the first Cornishfolk entered Michigan in the eighteenth century. Some writers have credited fur trader Alexander Henry with using Cornish miners when he attempted to develop copper deposits in Ontonagon County in the 1770s. Unfortunately, hard evidence is lacking. If the name fits the nationality there were two individuals named "Cornwall"

Cornish on Baffin Island

In 1577 and 1578 a number of Cornishmen joined Martin Frobisher's attempt at locating gold on Baffin Island. On the first expedition thirty of the ships' company were miners, refiners, and "appropriate civilians." When Eskimos were encountered and the English had difficulty with them, Nicholas Conger, "being a Cornishman and a good wrastler," grappled with an Eskimo and showed him "such a Cornish tricke, that he made his sides ake . . . for a month after." The Cornish miners filled three ships with ore and the fleet returned to England by way of Lands End, with the flagship putting in at Padstowe Road in Cornwall.

In 1578 few Cornish miners heeded the call to join Frobisher's expedition. As a result anyone available was impressed. The miners who survived the voyage loaded 1,350 tons of ore on thirteen ships. The *Gabriel* made the return voyage in a record twenty-two days, ending up in the Scilly Islands off Cornwall.

Possibly the reason that the Cornish miners refused to go on the second voyage was that the ore brought back to England proved to be worthless. They would save themselves for more profitable prospects in a more hospitable land.

who might have hailed from the county. John Cornwall arrived in Detroit as a private with Butler's Rangers as early as July 1779. In 1786 he entered into a contract with John Askin for farmland in the vicinity of modern Mt. Clemens, where he grew corn and other crops to sell to the community. Later he moved to the Canadian side of the Detroit River. Richard Cornwall was a native of New York and considered a master shipbuilder in the Great Lakes region. He lived in Detroit in 1796 and received some land along the St. Clair River from the Ojibwe.

By 1800 there were thousands of Cornish-Americans living in the United States, especially in the northeast quadrant. Large numbers of them had settled in upstate New York and New England. With the development of the Erie Canal after 1824, there was a grand migration to Michigan.

Beginning in the late eighteenth century and continuing into the first half of the nineteenth century conditions in Cornwall were in a state of flux. Life continued to center around mining. James Watt's refinement of the steam engine in 1790 allowed Richard Trevithick (1771–1833) to improve on

Watt's engine and design a steam-powered (Cornish) engine which could pump mines dry at great depths. As a result the mines were sunk deeper and the number of miners increased substantially. New ports were developed to ship ore. Around Camborne and Redruth, hundreds of buildings and chimneys began to appear. By 1850 nearly three-quarters of the world's supply of copper and half of its tin came from Cornwall and neighboring Devon.

Economically, the Cornish people began to face problems. Mining was based on many uncontrollable forces and the economy fluctuated with the prices of tin and copper. By the middle of the nineteenth century great deposits of tin and especially copper were discovered, and development began abroad. The deep, expensive Cornish mines could no longer financially compete with these new operations. The Cornish mines started a long decline.[4] Further complicating matters, in the 1840s Cornwall was hit with bad harvests.

Socially there were other problems confronting the people. During the decade between 1838 and 1848 there was a working-class movement for parliamentary reform (Chartism), which caused unrest. The considerable nonconformist religious ferment within the ranks of Cornish Methodism caused many to seek the "land of the free."

As a result, Cornish miners, an intelligent and independent group, were forced to leave their homeland during bad times for new homes and opportunities in the Americas, Australia, and South Africa. Here they were welcomed because of their work ethic and their mining expertise, which was in great demand. As a result, the successful development of mining in many parts of the world was directly connected to the emigrating Cornish miners. During the diaspora or "great migration" of the nineteenth century, a quarter of a million Cornish left their homeland.

Since difficult economic times touched many elements of Cornish life, some sought farms while the majority were attracted to the mining opportunities where their expertise was in demand in the United States. At first hundreds and then thousands migrated across the Atlantic. They settled in the iron mining areas of New York; the slate, shale, and coal mining areas of Pennsylvania; the lead mining areas of Wisconsin; and ultimately the copper and iron mining areas of the Lake Superior country.[5]

The Cornish who arrived in the United States had a unique character. Due to centuries of living on an isolated peninsula with their own language, the Cornish were exceedingly independent, and in a larger society they stuck together as a clan. They were a hardworking people who rarely mentioned the subject of wages and took on part-time employment to augment their meager wages, as they had as miners or fishermen in the Old Country.

The Cornish in Lower Michigan

Although the Cornish around the world are usually connected to mining, and indeed many Cornish in Michigan's Upper Peninsula found work in the copper and iron mines there, those who settled in the Lower Peninsula lived distinctly different lives from their brethren to the north. The first Cornish in southern Michigan were Cornish-Americans who hailed from New York and New England, who were quickly followed by Cornish immigrants arriving directly from their homeland. By the 1830s Macomb, Washtenaw, Lenawee, and Oakland counties in southern Michigan were the location of settlements of Cornish-Americans and newly arrived Cornish immigrants.[6] In the Pontiac area, William and Charlotte Stanlake settled what became a large farm, while Charles Parsons in neighboring Waterford was a farmer and carriage trimmer. By the 1850s Cornish farmers were living in Macomb and Oakland counties. Several members of the Trefly family, who were originally from Nova Scotia, settled on farms in Ingham County's Onondaga Township and Kinneville. Robert Treblecock, a Cornish immigrant, married in New York State and by 1856 was a farmer residing in London Township, Monroe County. He prospered in his new home and by 1870 had real estate valued at $2,500, and $900 in personal funds. By 1863, miners, some of them Cornishmen from Clifton in Keweenaw County, were "going below" to the Lower Peninsula to seek their fortunes.

In the 1860s and 1870s, members of the Rule family had settled on farms in the Thumb area. James Tredenick was a native of Pennsylvania whose career on the water took him from canal boatman to common sailor and then to a mate sailing the Atlantic. He left the sea around 1862 and settled in western Michigan, and after the autumn of 1879 he settled on a moderate-sized farm in Ionia County.[7] Little-known immigration of Cornish to rural Michigan continued. In 1911 the Moyle family left the Upper Peninsula mines and settled on a farm in Mattawan west of Kalamazoo.[8]

The Reynolds family of Cornwall had an interesting migration story that ended in Lower Michigan twice. Thomas and Mary Reynolds emigrated to New York City, and when they left the city, Thomas became a miner. Later he entered the seminary and became a Methodist minister, serving several congregations before his death at Port Huron. Due to her strong attachment to Cornwall, his wife, Mary, returned to her homeland. When he was old enough, their son John emigrated to London, Ontario, where he resided with an uncle. Later he found jobs in textile and woolen mills in Connecticut and Chicago. During the Civil War he paid two substitutes to serve in his place. In 1867 he moved to Jackson, Michigan, where he found employment at H. A. Hayden & Company's milling complex. Not satisfied with this occupation, John studied chemistry and biology and in the 1890s he was a food inspector for the city of Jackson.

With the development of the Michigan lumber industry, many more Cornishmen found employment in the state. Richard Trevidick went to East Saginaw in 1860, where he worked as a head sawyer in a number of sawmills. He purchased a sawmill and worked it with the help of his brother. When it burned in 1879 he moved to an eighty-acre farm where he raised his family. An unrelated Cornish-American, Henry Trevidick, was born in Mt. Clemens in 1846. First he worked in a planing mill in Saginaw and then in 1871 he settled at Clare, where he became a prominent merchant within the community. Civic-minded, he served as township treasurer and as school assessor.[9] Mary Treetick was an eighteen-year-old immigrant who was living with the Chandler family in Clinton Township, Macomb County in 1850. Although her occupation was not listed, probably she was a family servant. There was also ten-year-old Mary Trevick, also from Cornwall, who had been taken in by the Joshua Dickinson family, who were merchants. There was also a widow named Penrose residing in Berrien County in 1860.

Beginning in the early nineteenth century, a number of Cornish immigrants passed through Detroit en route to other Lower Peninsula locations, Wisconsin, or later the Upper Peninsula. Some of them decided to end their travels in Detroit and made the city their new home. Detroit attracted Cornish-Americans from rural areas as well. Names like Pasco, Pengelly, Pender, Rouse, Rowe, Tregaskis, Trevellech, and others appear in city records. A review of occupations provides a sense of their interests. Their occupations

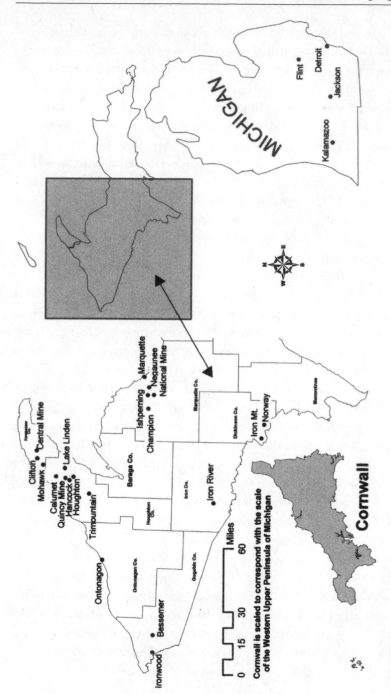

Cornish settlements in Michigan.

centered around industrial and technical jobs such as blacksmith, carpenter, crimper, draughtsman, engineer, machinist, molder, lithography printer, and wire weaver, to name a few. Others were in the service sector, working as clerks and porters. Cornish people worked as butchers, shoemakers, upholsterers, tailors, and harness makers. A few worked for the city fire and police departments. Still others worked for transportation companies. For example, Philip Tresize was a sailor and later a mate on a Great Lakes ship, while Ford A. Trevellick was an inspector with the U.S. Customs Service. In 1899 a number of Cornish-Americans gained local prominence. Samuel M. Trevellich was an attorney, Trebilcock and Brothers were jewelers, and Philip H. Tresize was a successful real estate agent. Other Trevellicks had moved to Ann Arbor and Benton Harbor.

The Cornish in the Upper Peninsula

Cornish Miners in the Upper Peninsula

As Cornwall was experiencing its mining problems, competition was developing in the Midwest. In the nineteenth century lead mining developed in the tri-state area of Illinois, Iowa, and Wisconsin, resulting in the need for expert miners. Mineral Point, Wisconsin, was established as a lead mining community in 1827, and Cornish deep rock miners began to arrive by the hundreds. By the time Douglass Houghton promoted the development of copper mining on the Keweenaw Peninsula in the 1840s, Cornish miners were beginning to be well established in the area.

When news of copper fever in Michigan spread to Wisconsin and the coal mines of Pennsylvania and other mining regions, Cornish people began to migrate to Michigan. From southwestern Wisconsin they migrated northward by way of the Mississippi, St. Croix, and Brulé rivers to the shore of Lake Superior. They traveled through wilderness and battled gnats, black flies, and mosquitoes. Others traveled by land and lake from Pennsylvania and other eastern communities, and from Canada, especially from Bruce Mine in Ontario, to reach upper Michigan.

New arrivals from Cornwall and elsewhere in the world were attracted by chain migration—that is, by letters about and publicity of the new region to Cornish communities. As early as the summer of 1845

Holman & Williams grocery store, Calumet, Michigan. Source: Candice S. Miller.

Cornish miners in the Copper Country wrote to the *London Miners' Journal* extolling the richness and excellent prospects of the newly opened copper mines in Michigan. This information was picked up by mining interests in Cornwall and elsewhere. The Cornish miners often discussed the value of these mines with the editor of the *Lake Superior News,* John Ingersoll, who noted this in his newspapers. This news was in turn picked up by other newspapers in the United States, and the news continued to spread. The fact that Cornish miners gave their nod to the value of these mines was reassuring to the local developers in the Copper Country.

The prosperity of America in general and specifically of the mining industry in America inspired many Cornish people to send letters to family and friends in the Old Country, where conditions were poor.[10] They also sent money or prepaid tickets to the Old Country to bring their friends and relatives to America. The *Marquette Mining Journal* noted in the summer of 1887 that the English of Ishpeming had sent home large accounts of money through banks and post offices.

As early as 1843–44 Jane and Job Masters had reached Copper Harbor. In the summer of 1844 Cornish miners working for the Lake Superior Mining

Company had sunk four shafts on the riverbank at Eagle River. A year later a group of Cornish miners were observed digging a shaft for a possible silver mine at Marquette's Presque Isle for the Lake Superior and New York Mining Company.[11] In 1846, there were Cornish miners working for the Boston and Lake Superior Mining Association, and at another location in the copper district, Captain Henry Clemo oversaw a group of Cornish miners. In 1847 when newspaper editor Horace Greeley visited Eagle Harbor he noted that there were some "Cousin Jacks"[12] living there, as well as at Cliff Mine.

The federal census of 1850 provides some insights into these new immigrants. However, while they were chiefly from Cornwall, the census listed them as "English," so speculation about the Cornish is necessary. At the time there were five Upper Peninsula counties—Chippewa, Michilimackinac, Marquette, Houghton, and Ontonagon. In the non-mining counties of Chippewa and Michilimackinac there were a small number of Englishmen involved in diverse occupations. It was a different story in the Copper Country. In Houghton County there were a total of 501 foreign-born residents. Of that number 261 (52 percent) were listed as "English." Their number included 122 miners and 15 laborers. There were 30 German miners out of 142 Germans in the area, and 18 Irish miners out of 59 Irishmen. There were 251 immigrants in Ontonagon County, of which 61 were of English origin. Of that number 33 were listed as miners. The next largest ethnic group among the miners was the Irish, with 28 miners, followed by the Germans, with 6. There were fewer Cornish miners in the Marquette Iron Range in the 1840s because they disdained the open pit operations and wanted to work underground.[13] It would be another thirty years before they would settle in large numbers on the Marquette Range as the mines went underground.

Cornish Communities in the Upper Peninsula

One of the important Cornish towns was Central Mine in Keweenaw County, which opened in 1854. The journal of schoolteacher Henry Hobart for 1863–64 provides a keen view of life in a community dominated by Cornish people. In fact, he refers to the area as "this land of Cornish manners," while others referred to it as Keweenaw's "Duchy of Corn wall." For many Cornish immigrants, life in this community was their introduction to American life. The immigrants boarded, rented, or owned their homes, and used their extra money to donate to church and schools, playing a major part in the community. In the process they assimilated but maintained their heritage as well. The Methodist Episcopal church was both a religious and a cultural center for the community.[14]

Within the mining communities of the Upper Peninsula, people usually lived in clusters of houses located near a mine shaft so that workers lived where they worked. Within these locations groups of people of common ethnicity tended to congregate, although many became mixed over the years.

Given the fact that many of the Cornishmen were mine captains and managers, their residences were connected with those of the mine officials. For instance, in Negaunee, the best residences were located on Main Street, where the wealthier people lived—the mining engineers, superintendents, and other salaried mine employees. The Cornish mining families followed the general pattern of living in mining locations. A vigorous location in Negaunee was known as Cornishtown. Originally the men living there worked in the Jackson Mine. Their houses were small cottages. Many added a garage with the coming of the automobile, and these garages were at times larger than the original house. The surrounding hills provided a good garden and hay land. Some families owned cows, which grazed on the hillsides and were kept in small barns during the winter. Mining families favored this location because it was close to the downtown area and was on the main highway to Ishpeming, where many men found jobs as the mines closed in Negaunee.

In the Copper Country, as larger mines like the Quincy and Calumet and Hecla developed later in the nineteenth century, Cornish miners followed their fortunes and moved to these areas. The Calumet & Hecla Mining Company, which was developed in 1864, attracted hundreds of Cornish miners and laborers. In 1871 there were 410 men working in the Calumet mine and 815 at the Hecla mine. The rich Calumet conglomerate copper ore impressed these Cornish miners and they often referred to its value and importance in dialectical stories.

Over the years conditions in the Copper Country changed, and by 1910, while there was still a sizeable Cornish population there, many had left for other opportunities. In 1899–1900 at Calumet, out of a total population of 20,000, there were 3,500 Cornish (17.5 percent). The Finns and native-born Americans dominated the scene with 5,000 people each, amounting to a combined 50 percent of the population. At Mohawk, ten miles to the north of

Calumet, the Cornish comprised 30 percent of the population of 3,000, and at Wolverine, two miles northeast of Calumet, there was a Cornish enclave in which Cornishmen numbered 800 of 1,500 people (53.3 percent), comprising the largest ethnic group at the mine.

Available statistics provide additional insights into the Cornish miners of the Copper Country. Before coming to the United States 60 percent of the Cornish were miners, while 10 percent were general laborers. Many of the first Cornishmen who came to America occupied positions as foremen and bosses and as a result were drawing salaries between $85 and $125 per month; Cornish employees received an average weekly wage of $14.90—the highest paid to ethnic employees. Employers felt that the Cornish were the most adaptable and most efficient employees and made the best citizens.[15]

Iron Ranges

There are three iron ranges in Michigan: the Marquette, Menominee, and Gogebic Iron Ranges. The first mining on the Marquette Range began in 1844. The greatest Cornish immigration to the Marquette Range took place between 1856 and 1885, and especially after 1874 with the sinking of the first shafts and the development of underground mining. Prior to this time, Cornish miners tended to avoid the Marquette Range because ore was mined by the open pit system and this was not a traditional form of mining for them. After shafts were sunk, Cornish miners were attracted to the range from other areas in the state like the Copper Country and directly from the Old Country.

Between 1880 and 1890 the introduction of mining machines and the steam shovel (in 1889) changed conditions around the mines. A labor strike in 1895 drove many Cornishmen and others from the range to mines in Montana, Colorado, and Nevada. In a report issued by an anonymous mining company on the Marquette Range in 1898, the Cornish comprised 25 percent of the employees, while by 1909 their number had been reduced to 13.5 percent. There were also fewer Cornish immigrants leaving the Old Country. The Cornishmen who remained in the mines were those who held skilled positions or were employed as foremen, as managers, or in some other executive capacity.

Although Cornish miners arrived early in the development of the mines on the Marquette Range and many had left by 1890, others continued to be attracted to the range. Chain migration caused many Cornish miners who came from places like Redruth and Camborne to settle in Negaunee to work in the iron mines early in the twentieth century.

The Menominee Iron Range, which ran from Norway and Vulcan on the east through Iron Mountain to Crystal Falls and Iron River on the west, was opened in 1874 and flourished when the Iron Mountain mine opened in 1879. The first miners were Cornishmen who moved from the Marquette Range because the new range was believed to offer better opportunities in regard to both advancement and working conditions. For several years after development began on the Menominee Range there was very active immigration from Cornwall. After 1889 very few Cornishmen entered the mines, and many of the older men moved to other mining districts in the West. Labor strikes in 1893 and 1895 further caused many Cornishmen to migrate out of the range.

By 1909 the Cornish comprised only 5 percent of the ten thousand people living in the Iron Mountain district, while in Norway and Vulcan they barely made up one-tenth of one percent of the total population of nine thousand; the same was true at Iron River and Crystal Falls. Besides the above-mentioned reasons for outward migration, second-generation Cornish-Americans were no longer going into underground mining. If their fathers were working as foremen, superintendents or captains, and bosses, they secured positions as managers and office staff.

The Gogebic Range was opened in the far western Upper Peninsula in 1884. The first miners were Cornishmen who went from the Marquette and Menominee Ranges and from Cornwall itself. Then in 1894 an outmigration began, and three years later immigration from Cornwall began to decline. As a result, after 1895 the Cornish no longer dominated the field. In 1909 on the Gogebic Range the Cornish comprised 494 men out of 2,800 total employed on the range.

Mining Techniques and Equipment

Cornish miners brought with them expertise, lore, techniques, and tools related to mining. As a result they had a great impact on Michigan and American mining. The Cornish made the best mining captains. The mine captain's job was to observe and study the progress of the mine's workings; a mine captain was almost by intuition able to follow the crazy

Cornish mining captains and miners were found in the copper and iron mines of the Upper Peninsula and in the coal mines of the Lower Peninsula.

convolutions of the rock formations and ore bodies. Mine captains took pride in getting the ore out with the least expense, avoiding taking out waste rock, and protecting the safety of the miners under their charge. Although they were trained in colleges as mining engineers, experienced geologists knew to follow the directions of the Cornish captains regarding the location, nature, and position of ore bodies. The miners held the captains in high esteem, and when a captain entered a drift, the men would stop work to show their deference. On the surface the miners would touch their caps and address them as "captain."

Over the years, a few Cornish captains owned and operated their own mines. The Negaunee Mine located to the southeast of Negaunee was a small-scale operation developed by Captain Samuel Mitchell in 1887. It was eventually incorporated into the Cleveland Cliffs operation.

The captains contributed their expertise to improve mining methods. Captain Collick was known for his invention of the Cleveland-Cliffs Sheet-Iron Sconce (Cornish for candlestick), a device for shielding the candle flame on the miner's cap. Other Cornish miners on the Marquette Range became famous for their physical strength and their ability to wrestle, handle a drill, or load more ore than others in the mine.

They also introduced "Cornish stamps," a simple but widely used milling technology for crushing ores. Consisting of iron-shod wooden hammers mounted on wooden shafts, which were raised by water or steam power and then dropped, the Cornish mill was well suited to small mines and isolated areas where expensive machinery could not easily be imported. Improvements made upon the Cornish stamp eventually led, by the 1860s, to the growing adoption of the steam-powered stamp, which used all-iron hammers and shafts and steam pressure rather than gravity for the crushing stroke.

Cornish engineers developed an efficient and reliable modification of the Watt steam-powered pumping engine in the early nineteenth century especially for mining purposes. Called the Cornish pump, it had found wide use in the Lake Superior mining districts by the end of the 1860s.

The reciprocal motion of the steam engine could also be used for other purposes. As mines in the copper districts of the Upper Peninsula began to go hundreds of feet below the earth's surface, conventional ladders became increasingly troublesome as a means of going to and coming from working areas. This led some mines to install another Cornish mining technology: the man engine. Similar to an escalator, a man engine had small platforms mounted six to eight feet apart on a shaft that a steam engine moved up and down. By alternately moving from these platforms to stationary platforms mounted on the side of a mine shaft (or to a second parallel moving shaft with similar platforms), miners could move to and from subterranean working areas much more quickly and with less effort than by using ladders.

A common question at the mines was whether the miner should be paid for the tonnage or the footage removed. The Cornish stoping contract allowed each miner to contract with the mine captain for the work he had to do. This was based on the footage of ore removed. Coming from a seabound peninsula, the Cornish miners used the term *cubic fathom* (six feet) as the basic unit of measurement. The concept was introduced in the 1850s and persisted for nearly seventy years in many mines in Michigan. Although the fathom was more or less vaguely interpreted, the contract was generally based on footage drilled per shift, each shift being an individual contract of material removed by an individual. By this system the holes were directed to best advantage under the strict supervision of mine captains. This system allowed more ore than rock to be removed from the mine.

*A Cornish contribution to mining, the man engine allowed miners to efficiently and rap-
idly descend into or exit the mine. This photograph was taken at Quincy Mine, Hancock,
Michigan, in the 1880s. Source: Superior View Photography, Marquette, Michigan.*

Other Cornish innovations in the mines included drilling by hand with
sledges, blasting with black powder and later dynamite, and hauling a Cornish
"kibble" (bucket or skip), powered by a Cornish horse-drawn whim (the capstan used in raising ore for smaller operations).

Cornish immigrants also introduced medical services. Owners of the
Cliff Mine first imported the "bal" surgeon system from Cornwall. In return
for one dollar paid per month from married men and fifty cents from bach-
elors, the company agreed to have its surgeon look after the men and their
families. This practice became widespread throughout the mining region.
Cornish miners have been credited with spurring the creation of the Calumet
& Hecla Hospital in 1870.

Child Labor in the Mines

Many of the Cornish miners who came to Michigan began their mining
careers in Cornwall as young as twelve years old. As a result, it was not

uncommon to find similarly aged lads working in the mines in the Copper Country. On February 18, 1864, at the Clifton Mine, thirteen-year-old Henry Benney slipped and was killed while his father watched in horror. At the same time, Henry Hobart, the teacher at Clifton, noted that because of a slowdown in mining activity, the young washboys would be back in elementary school. In 1895 a fifteen-year-old Cornish lad was killed in the Osceola Mine fire. In these early years there were no child labor laws and these children's wages augmented the family income, and thus the practice was fairly common.

Demographics

Cornish Migration around and out of Michigan

A little-known and understood aspect of life in nineteenth-century America was the ongoing movement of people around the country, and immigrants were a part of this. If the Cornish migrated from Wisconsin's lead mines and the coalfields of Pennsylvania to Michigan, what was to keep them in Michigan?

From the earliest days of Cornish emigration, Cornish miners found that with their expertise they could find better positions in developing mining areas throughout the country and the world. As early as 1863 miners from Clifton were leaving for California, Pike's Peak in Colorado, and South America. At other times the loss of jobs or reduction of wages caused many to leave the state. Although it is difficult to get a head count of men leaving the Michigan mines, in July 1892 the *Marquette Mining Journal* provided a measure. According to this newspaper, in June 1892 the South Shore Railroad in Ishpeming sold more than $600 worth of tickets per day, while in the first week of July, during a downturn at the mines, they sold more than $4,000 in tickets.

Within Michigan Cornishmen moved frequently between the different mining districts. In the Upper Peninsula, as the iron ranges of Menominee and Gogebic opened in the 1880s, Cornishmen from the established areas moved there. During the nineteenth century the great bituminous coal basin in the central part of the Lower Peninsula was gradually developed. The great impetus to Saginaw coal mining dated from 1895 and was stimulated by the decline of the timber industry, which had previously been the main source of fuel for the extraction of salt. Mines were developed in Bay and Genesee counties to the north and south. The pillar and chamber system of mining was practically the only one used. The labor force for these mines came from many districts, and more than half of them were Americans. Those not native-born had lived an average of sixteen years in the United States. Some Cornish miners found their way to these mines. One of them, Thomas Pengilley, worked in the area during the heyday of coal mining from 1903 until 1922. The coal mines flourished into the 1920s, but the poor quality of the coal caused the industry to go into a slump, and many of these miners moved south to Flint and Detroit and found jobs in the auto industry.[16]

Cornishmen also found mining positions outside of Michigan. They migrated to the iron ranges in northern Minnesota and found positions in the mines and mills of Anaconda and Butte, Montana; others migrated to California. Cornish people dominated Grass Valley, California, and there was a large Cornish community working the silver mines of Virginia City, Nevada. Others moved from the copper mines of Arizona to Utah or from the coal mines of Alabama back to Michigan. Besides the mines in the United States, there was also a demand for miners in Canada, Mexico, Brazil, Chile, and South Africa. Newspaper accounts in Michigan provide a scattered but interesting account of these migrating Cornishmen.

A review of the *Marquette Mining Journal* illustrates this internal migration. Edward Moyle, an early settler in Negaunee and one of the early employees of the Jackson mine, moved to Butte, Montana, in 1890. Ben Williams left Negaunee in 1894 for Lead, South Dakota, and in the spring of 1905 James Tonkin and his son William migrated to Austin, Nevada, where James's brother, William, was located and had secured jobs for them. At the time there were other men in Negaunee who were also talking of going to the Silver State.

If the immigrants themselves did not migrate from Michigan over the years, their children certainly did. When Cornish immigrant Captain Thomas Buzzo died in August 1913, his family was scattered across the

Beginning in 1919, hundreds of Cornishmen from the Upper Peninsula and elsewhere were attracted to Flint, where they along with other ethnics found jobs in the Buick plant, seen here during a noon hour rush around 1929. Source: Superior View Studio.

United States and Canada. The Minnesota iron ranges had attracted his son Arthur, a mining captain, to Ely, and a married daughter to neighboring Virginia, Minnesota. Two other sons lived in Salt Lake City and Chicago. Two other married daughters and one single daughter lived in Ishpeming, while another resided in British Columbia. The copper city of Butte, Montana, attracted two married daughters.[17] This type of internal migration was common not only to Cornish people but to immigrants of many nationalities.

As with other immigrants, Cornish people regularly moved around the United States and even traveled to the Old Country. There are many newspaper accounts of Cornishmen returning to the Old Country in the late 1890s to spend anywhere from two to four months visiting family and friends and enjoying the more moderate climate of Cornwall. Within the United States many Cornish people regularly traveled by train to visit family and friends throughout Michigan and in other states.

Labor

Cornish miners were always seen as an independent group of rugged indi-
vidualists. The stoping contract, introduced by the Cornish, was a system
whereby each miner contracted with his mine captain for the work he had
to do. Given their expertise in mining and the fact that many of them were
mine bosses, superintendents, and managers, the Cornish generally were
not attracted to radical union groups. However, throughout the nineteenth
century there were many instances where Cornish miners or their bosses
went on strike because of low or unpaid wages, brutal bosses, or poor working conditions. Still, these were usually isolated cases.

During the 1913-14 Michigan copper strike in the Copper Country,
Cornishmen were found on both sides of the struggle. There was Houghton
County sheriff James A. Cruse and deputy sheriff John Chellow, who heavy-
handedly enforced the law and became quite unpopular with the strikers.
Since the mining captains often represented the mining companies, many
were threatened and attacked by members of the Western Federation of
Miners (WFM). However, there were also many Cornish strikers, like Sydney
Thomas, who was president of the WFM local in Ahmeek, and local labor
union leaders, like William Williams, E. James Rowe, and James Paull.[18]

During the strike from July 1913 to April 1914, some 2,500 miners left the
Copper Country, many of them never to return. At one point about 200 min-
ers returned to Cornwall, some blaming the WFM and praising the Calumet
& Hecla Mining Company.

Not all labor issues took place in mining communities. One of the
most famous Cornish labor leaders in Michigan was Richard F. Trevellick (1830–95), who was born in the Scilly Islands and was profoundly
influenced by the evangelical brand of Methodism and its related social
justice movements, to which his family adhered. Between 1851 and 1858
he was a seaman. During the Civil War, being a lifelong abolitionist, he
refused service in the Confederate Army. He then settled in New York and
finally settled in Detroit, where he joined Detroit's Shipcarpenter's and
Caulkers' Local 4 and became its president in 1865. He quickly became
involved in labor agitation. In 1864 he was a Detroit Trades Assembly
delegate to the Louisville, Kentucky, convention that created the International Industrial Assembly of North America, an abortive attempt at a

national labor federation. He was also active in the Michigan Grand Eight Hours League. In 1867 he attended conventions that led to the founding of the National Labor Union (NLU), the first national trades federation of the post-Civil War period. He also co-founded the secretive Industrial Brotherhood. Although the latter was short-lived and ineffective, its statement of principles, written by Trevellick, was adopted nearly verbatim by the Knights of Labor (KOL) in 1878. Trevellick traveled extensively throughout the West, South, and the anthracite coalfields of the Mid-Atlantic region. He is credited with founding more than two hundred local unions and three statewide trades assemblies.

In 1909, when Cornish and non-Cornish mining captains and superintendents organized on the Mesabi Range in Minnesota, there was talk that similar actions might take place on the Marquette Iron Range. Later, this loose-knit organization primarily met to discuss problems of underground mine safety.

Occupations

Traditionally, Cornishmen were involved in mining. In the 1890s Cornishmen in Michigan were engineers, drill boys, teamsters, masons, oilers, machinists, miners, and bosses, while others were copper washers and copper dressers. However, times changed. As newer immigrants entered the Upper Peninsula many Cornishmen moved to the Far West and elsewhere where their skills were in demand. Many of them left mining and found new occupations.

In addition to working mines, Cornishmen thrived as entrepreneurs throughout Michigan, and especially in the Upper Peninsula. James Rasewarn was born in Cornwall in 1835 and migrated to the Lake Superior region in 1855. For the next quarter century he lived in the Copper Country, before going to South America and then returning to the Upper Peninsula. At forty-six years of age he purchased the Eagle Harbor Hotel and left the world of mining.[19]

There were numerous Cornish businessmen located throughout the Upper Peninsula by the late nineteenth century. George Trevillian had a fruit and confectionery shop that also sold tobacco and cigars at 351 N. 5th Street in Calumet. After an early career in mining (1888–94) John F. Cowling developed a successful general store business in Iron Mountain. In 1902 James Trevarrow operated a store in Iron Mountain selling general merchandise and millinery, while in neighboring Quinesec A. J. Trevarthan was selling patent medicines, tobacco, and candy. William Trebilcock in 1909 was a major concrete contractor in Ishpeming and did extensive work for the city on streets, sidewalks, and structures.

Not all Cornishmen engaged in some form of mining job or became businessmen, however. Some, like Thomas A. Trevethan, born in Cornwall in 1836, became involved in agriculture. During his early years Trevethan was engaged in mining and foundation construction at mill sites before he was placed in charge of the Huron stamp mill. Between 1864 and 1877 he became one of the leading general merchants in Houghton. However, at forty-one years of age he purchased a tract of heavily timbered land adjoining Chassell and began a new career. Half of his four-hundred-acre parcel was soon cleared and in a high state of cultivation. There were other farmers like Thomas Trewarthon, James Vial, and William Williams who operated farms in Chassell, Portage, and Schoolcraft townships. There were also a number of Cornish farmers in Saginaw and a dairyman at Cornishtown in Negaunee.

Women

The Upper Peninsula was a hard land, especially for women, where the amenities of life were few. In the early 1850s Rebecca Jewell Francis was listed in the census. She had been given the Ojibwe name Swangideed Wayquay, or Lady Unafraid, because of her courage in braving the frontier and its notorious winters. Furthermore, she taught general education to the local Native American population.

A woman's traditional role was to stay at home, keep house, and raise families. In the early days of Cornish settlement in Michigan, women had to improvise to adjust to the frontier conditions of the mining districts. Many married women had large families, so that much of their time was spent on family chores such as washing laundry, making and repairing clothing, preparing food, and cooking meals.

There were few industrial outlets in the mining districts where women, even if they and their husbands were so inclined, could find employment. Some women found that they could bring in additional wages to their families by taking in boarders. Boarders were often close family relatives, and it

The Lutey Family and Flowers

Cornwall, located far to the south in the British Isles, is known for its mild climate and beautiful flower gardens. The Lutey family, who hailed from Penzance, came to Michigan as flower growers and merchants. The children of Joseph Lutey (1830–87), a groundskeeper for a large estate in Penzance—Henry, Richard, Albert, James, and Samuel—operated a series of successful florist shops and greenhouses in the Copper Country during the first decade of the twentieth century. In following years they and family members operated similar shops in Ironwood, Ishpeming, and eventually Marquette. Other members of the family opened shops in Detroit as well.

was not uncommon to have family squabbles add to the tension of living in closely crowded quarters. In 1860 a boarder was typically charged $10 per month or $120 per year, and in 1864 the price rose five dollars. If a boarding house served "Yankee style" food, the price often climbed to as much as $20–$25 per month.

One woman who successfully opened her home to boarders was Johanna Rawlings. Her husband Joseph was a prominent engineer and mechanic at Clifton in the early 1860s. Despite the fact that she had seven children and needed several servants, she opened her large frame house to the local teacher, Henry Hobart. She maintained a cow for fresh milk for her family, processed geese and chickens for meals, and was constantly hostile toward the young servant girls she hired because they did not meet her expectations.

Since it was possible that a Cornish miner would be an itinerant, moving to other mining locations in the United States, daughters were often separated from their families when they followed their husbands to new work sites. In the twentieth century, many Cornish-American girls married and then moved to Grass Valley, California, or Butte, Montana, with their husbands. Such moves were permanent unless conditions in the Michigan mines improved and the family returned to the Upper Peninsula.

First-generation women were strictly mothers and housewives. Many women in the next generation worked until marriage, and then stayed home to raise their families. However, there were a few women who were listed

in the 1920 census as "dressmaker at home" or as "seamstress." A few were
housekeepers for other families. Seventy-nine-year-old widow Elizabeth
Carlyon was one of the few women listed in the census as living on her "own
income."

By the 1880s and 1890s some of the young Cornish-American girls had
been born in the United States. Anne Trevorrow was a dressmaker who operated out of her boarding house. At Hancock, Mary J. Penprase, a widow, took
in boarders, and her daughter Amelia was a dressmaker. In Detroit in 1889,
Catherine E. Pasco, a widow, was a dressmaker. Later in the 1920s women
found positions as salesladies at Kern's Department Store, clerks with the
Postal Tel-Cable Company, stenographers with the public library, fitters for
Crowley Sisters Corset Shop, and dental assistants. These were a few of the ac-
ceptable female occupations in bustling 1920s Detroit. Women found similar
jobs in countless communities throughout southern Michigan, in cities like
Jackson, Flint, and Kalamazoo.

Two Cornish-American sisters, Ella Mae Penglase (1858–1950) and Jenny
M. Penglase (1872–1941), played an important role in the field of education in
Iron Mountain. They were born in Calumet and moved with their parents to
Iron Mountain, where they were considered pioneer residents. Ella was one
of the first teachers in the Iron Mountain schools (1884–1918). She retired in
1918 and joined with her sister Jenny to become co-owner and operator of
the Penglase Business College in Iron Mountain. It remained in operation
until 1946.[20]

Many immigrant women were familiar with medicinal plants and traditional medicine that could prevent some ailments. Susanna Sleep Morcom
was one such traditional medicine practitioner. Trained as a nurse in the Old
Country, she was also a practitioner of "the old knowledge" of Cornwall. While
in Montana, Ironwood, Michigan, and then Detroit she kept her medicinal
ingredients in a miner's dinner pail and served as a midwife. There were also
women and men who had the gift of "healing hands," who provided a calming
effect to others through massage.[21]

Cornish woman found that if they were careful with their time they could
find recreation outside the home. They would visit with family and neighbors
and attend picnics in the summer. The Methodist church offered a variety of
social organizations, including the Ladies' Aid Society, temperance groups,
and the church choir. Minnie Uren, for example, was the church organist in

Louise Holman, with her twin sons Merton and Milton, 1922, was typical of hundreds of Cornish women who accompanied their husbands to the Upper Peninsula and made a new home for their families. Source: Holman Family and St. George's Day.

Negaunee in 1905. In July 1903 the Ladies' Aid Society of Mitchell Methodist Church in Negaunee gave a house social and lawn party. The event consisted of ice cream, cake, and an informal program of vocal and instrumental music. Outside the church, Daughters of St. George lodges, which were found in most Cornish communities, attracted many Cornish women. An auxiliary of the Sons of St. George, the Daughters provided labor for the Good Friday and St. George Day community dinners. Cornish women were also members of women's auxiliaries of the Masons and other feminine organizations.

Sons of Immigrants

Many of the sons of Cornish immigrants took divergent career routes from those of their fathers. Michael and Lydia Abrams had seven children. Two of their sons, Edward and James, became prominent physicians and surgeons in Hancock and Calumet. In addition Edward had a statewide reputation and received many literary honors. He was considered the leading authority on Cornish history, traditions, and customs in the state of Michigan in 1911.

Samuel Eddy was born in Cornwall in 1869 and emigrated to Michigan with his parents. He graduated from Michigan State Normal School (now Eastern Michigan University) in 1888 and went on to teach school. Eventually he became involved in real estate, bought timbered lands, and with a partner operated a sawmill at Torch Lake. J. Arthur Minnear, the son of Cornish immigrants, engaged in the general brokerage business in Laurium in the early twentieth century.

By 1930 in the Copper Country many second-generation Cornish-Americans had left the mines and found employment in non-mining fields. The census and city directories show them as mail carriers, drivers for Cudahy Packing Co., washmen for Needham Brothers Laundry, barbers, assistant supervisors and linemen for the Houghton County Electric Light Company, teachers, special delivery managers, printers, and weighmasters for People's Fuel Company. Few of the younger generation became miners. John Polglaze was a deputy sheriff of the Quincy Mine as a "location caretaker." At Trimountain a fellow Cornishman was a blacksmith for the Copper Range Company. In 1936 Harry Vivian, a graduate of Michigan Technological University and chief engineer at Calumet & Hecla Consolidated Copper, was a director on the board of the Ishpeming Gold Mining Company.

Culture

Politics

Local and state politics attracted many Cornish immigrants. The early county records of the Copper Country and the three iron ranges show many Cornish immigrants serving as constables, supervisors, clerks, justices of the peace, education inspectors, and mine inspectors, to mention just a few. Later many would serve as mayors and city officials as well. Their children continued to serve in similar capacities.

A number of Upper Peninsula Cornish immigrants served in the state legislature. Captain William Harris, who was born in 1818, came to Michigan in 1846 and was a miner and a very successful mining captain. By 1860 he developed new businesses, including several stores, a dock, and warehouse. He was interested in politics, and between 1871 and 1875 he served in the Michigan legislature representing Ontonagon County.

Thomas B. Dunstan (1850–1902) accompanied his parents from Camborne when he was three years old. He attended Lawrence University in Appleton, Wisconsin, and the University of Michigan law school and was admitted to the bar in Keweenaw County in 1872. He was soon elected judge of probate and became prosecuting attorney for Keweenaw County. In 1879 he moved to Pontiac, then returned to Central Mine in 1882. Soon after, he was elected to the state legislature; he was a delegate to the Republican National Convention in Chicago in 1886, and was elected to the state senate in 1889. Dunstan was elected by a large majority as lieutenant governor in 1896–97; after he completed his term he returned to his law practice in Hancock. Besides his political career, Dunstan was president and director of a number of mining companies and banks. He was also appointed to the Michigan Technological University Board of Trustees and was an active member of the Historical Society of Michigan.

Many others served at the town, township, and county levels. Captain George Brewer worked as a boy in the mines of Cornwall before he emigrated to America in 1866. He worked for three years at Bruce Mine in Ontario and then at a number of mines in Negaunee. When the Gogebic Range opened, he traveled west. In addition to being a mine captain, he was engaged in the furniture business and served as deputy mine inspector. In 1907 he was elected to the position of mine inspector of Gogebic County.

Peter W. Pasco was born in Porkellis, Cornwall, in 1854. He settled in Republic, Michigan, where he served as assistant superintendent until 1884 and then as underground captain for the Republic Iron Mining Company. Around 1903 he served as clerk of Republic Township and then for two years held the office of township treasurer.

A miner turned farmer, Thomas Trevethan was also engaged in politics. He cast his first ballot for President Lincoln and for many years was a member of the Houghton County Republican committee. He was also a member of the Portage township board and alderman of the village of Houghton. He was one of the organizers of Chassell Township in 1888, was its first supervisor, and was reelected for a second term.

John Reynolds worked in a textile mill before becoming a Jackson city food inspector. In 1881 he was elected to the city council, where he played an extremely active role in city government.

In the twentieth and twenty-first centuries, Cornish-Americans have continued to play active roles in local, state, and national politics and government. One of the more prominent members of state government was Candice Miller, the descendant of Cornish immigrants to the Copper Country. A resident of St. Clair Shores, Michigan, she worked her way through the political maze and in 1994 was elected as Michigan's fortieth (and first female) secretary of state. She was reelected to this position in 1998. Unable to run again for that office, Ms. Miller ran for the U.S. House of Representatives and won the election in 2002.

Religion

During the eighteenth century, Cornwall was the scene of preaching by John Wesley (1703–91), the father of Methodism, and many Cornish people were attracted to Methodism. Cornish immigrants brought a strong attachment to Methodism with them to the New World.

As a result, when Cornish people moved into an area or community, they soon established a Methodist church. The adjacent towns of Phoenix and Central Mine are examples of this type of development. The village of Phoenix was established in 1843–44 and a Methodist church was established soon after. It continued to hold services until the late 1920s. At Eagle Harbor a Cornish Methodist congregation was organized during the winter of 1846–47, and as more Cornish people arrived new churches were opened. The Central Mine Methodist Episcopal church was opened in 1869 and was active until it closed in 1903. Still standing, its simple architectural style mirrors that which appeared in Cornwall in the fifteenth century.

Religion was an important part of the lives of the Cornish people. Many Cornish individuals preached at Sunday services and others became Methodist ministers, missionaries, and social workers. Reverend Frank Dye was born in 1875 in Cornwall and in 1893 attended the Moody Bible Institute in Chicago. He first served a Congregational church in Iron Mountain and was known for his plain-language sermons. During his fifty-year ministry he was a guest preacher at many seminaries, colleges, and universities. He eventually founded the Los Angeles Wilshire Boulevard Congregational Church.

Reverend John Strike was born in 1872 at Porthleven, Cornwall, and worked as a fisherman after his father's death. In 1893 he arrived in Michigan, worked as miner, saved his money, and entered Albion College. After his graduation he served Methodist congregations in Michigamme and Champion, and between 1912 and 1962 he was pastor of the Centennial Church at Calumet.[22]

In the Lower Peninsula numerous clergymen served the various Methodist congregations. Reverend Richard Pengilly was born in Cornwall and by the 1870s was serving as pastor of the Methodist Episcopal church in

Nashville in downstate Barry County. In 1881 Reverend William Chapple, a Cornwall native, greatly strengthened the Methodist congregation at Bridgeport, outside of Saginaw, through his ministry. In the twentieth century, Reverend Billy Morcom served congregations in Michigan, moved out west, and then served as a Methodist missionary in Alaska. The list of Cornish-American ministers, missionaries, and social workers is long, and these men merely highlight the strong and deep religiosity of the Cornish people.

Culinary Customs

The Cornish brought a number of foodways with them, but the Cornish pasty is the most easily identified with the Upper Peninsula and the Cornish immigrant. Legend has it that the devil would never dare cross the River Tamar for fear of ending up as a filling in a Cornish pasty. Over the centuries a variety of ingredients have gone into the pasty crust.

The pasty is a hearty and nourishing food that miners took into the mines with them and warmed on a shovel over a candle. American chronicler John Forster wrote of the custom, saying that when the Cornishman went to dine, he said, "I must take my meat," and warmed his coffee and pasty with the candle on his hat. Forster continued:

> A "paasty" is an enormous turn-over, filled with chopped beefsteak, boiled potatoes and onions with spice. This strong dish is immensely satisfying. It is the Cornishman's great backer, but no American should indulge in the toothsome "paasty" at a late hour unless he should desire to have called up in his dreams, ghosts of his forefathers, in unlimited succession.[23]

Though it is a relatively simple dish, there are heated debates over what constitutes a "traditional" pasty. This freestanding pie is usually composed of diced or ground beef, potatoes, and onions. The introduction of carrots and rutabagas remains controversial. Culinary writers Jane and Michael Stern talk about this controversy in *Real American Food:*

> Serious gastroethnographers distinguish between a true Upper Peninsula Cornish pasty, made with cubes of steak, and a Finnish-style UP pasty, made with ground beef and pork. Further debate swirls around issues such as

whether the dough should be made with lard or suet; and the filling—with or without rutabaga; and the crimp of the crust—at the top or along the side edge.[24]

The pasty was consumed not only by miners, but also by Cornish families as their main meal. Every Cornish housewife had her own special pasty recipe. The pasty remains popular in the Upper Peninsula today, and is still seen as a traditional Cornish-American food.

More than a century and a half after its introduction, the pasty has been accepted by many in the Upper Peninsula, and shops selling the pasty can be found in the Lower Peninsula as well. Some people will argue that the pasty is actually a traditional Finnish food! Only in the Upper Peninsula can the designation "Pasty Shop" be found in the Yellow Pages. Pasties are sold fresh or frozen from pasty shops that dot the roadsides from Ironwood to St. Ignace. As with many Upper Peninsula foods, pasties have become so popular with visitors that they are shipped throughout the United States as well.

The pasty was not the only food introduced by the Cornish. Other Cornish fare includes heavy cake, plum pudding, scalded or clotted cream, figgy duff, saffron bread or buns, and seedy biscuits. Many of these traditional foods continue to be eaten by third- and fourth-generation Cornish-Americans.

Sports

Cornish immigrants introduced a number of unique sports to Michigan. The game of cricket expanded in England in the eighteenth century, and by 1773 was being played in Devon and also in neighboring Cornwall.[25] The interest in cricket continued to spread and when the English and Cornish settled in the United States in the nineteenth century they brought the game to Michigan. Cricket was first introduced in Detroit with the establishment of the Peninsula Cricket Club in 1858. Members of the club played on grounds located on Woodward Avenue. By 1885 the club's officers were primarily English in origin. Cricket was popular on the East Coast in the nineteenth century, and by 1890 there was a cricket league playing major East Coast and Midwest cities, including Detroit.

Many of the Cornish who settled in the Upper Peninsula were skilled players and organized cricket teams, especially in the Copper Country.

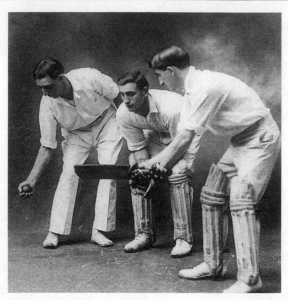

Cricket players "in action." Kearsarge Mine, Michigan. 1912. Source: Tom Friggens.

On the Marquette Iron Range, on Saturday afternoon, July 16, 1892, the Sir Humphrey Davy Lodge of the Sons of St. George played a Marquette team and won by four wickets. Little is recorded of other cricket games, as baseball was becoming the sport of choice throughout the Upper Peninsula. However, the Cornish and other people of British origin continued to play the game with which they were familiar. In 1908 there was talk of a cricket series between the English Oak and North of England teams along with eight teams in the Copper Country. A year later a cricket club was organized in Negaunee with the intention of league play with teams in the Copper Country from Calumet, Tamarack, Kearsarge, Ahmeek, Quincy, Mohawk, Trimountain, and Painesdale. Unfortunately, little information about the local games appears in the *Marquette Mining Journal* due to the lack of popular interest. Cricket died out with World War I but around 1923 there was an attempt at reviving the game in the Copper Country. Today it is virtually an unknown sport in the United States.[26]

Wrestling was an important facet of Cornish life and was described in detail in Richard Carew's survey of Cornwall in 1602.[27] Due to work in the mines, the average Cornish miner developed a strong build. Barefooted, the

Cornish wrestlers in their traditional canvas jackets, Gwinn, Michigan, probably ca. 1910. Source: Superior View Photography.

wrestler wore a special canvas jacket with a wide canvas belt tied firmly in front. The starting "holt" was a vice-like grip on the opponent's lapels—and from there it was each man for himself.

Cornish wrestling tournaments were frequently held for Sons of St. George celebrations like St. George's Day and the summer reunion. They were also held for the Fourth of July and as exhibitions. The communities of Ahmeek in Houghton County and Negaunee in Marquette County had special facilities with bleachers for the grand exhibitions held there. At Ahmeek, which was a center of wrestling, there was seating for two thousand spectators, and wrestling tournaments were held under the auspices of the Ahmeek Athletic Association. In 1916 they held some of the most successful tournaments in the Copper Country.

Cornish wrestling became so popular that men of other nationalities learned its techniques and competed. Some Cornish wrestlers moved into regular wrestling.[28] Jack Carkeek (1861–1924), who had started Cornish wrestling in 1877 in Michigamme, by 1909 had a national reputation not only in Cornish wrestling but in the catch-as-catch-can and Greco Roman styles as well. After running into trouble with the law in San Francisco, California, Carkeek dropped from the scene.[29]

Another sporting activity popular among Cornish-Americans was hammer-and-drill contests. The contests were the pride of the ethnic group and held as part of the Fourth of July celebration. Three-man teams from the various mines would pound away at huge blocks of rock. The team that could drill the deepest in a given period of time won a barrel of beer. There was such avid interest in hammer-and-drill contests that the *Marquette Mining Journal* published the results of the contests in Butte, Montana, where many Upper Peninsula Cornishmen had migrated.

People

Cornish Relations with Other Nationalities

The Cornish came to the Michigan mining country speaking the English language and possessing the expertise needed to work in the mines. As a result, they obtained the best positions in the mines, while others with fewer skills or arriving later were forced to take lower positions. The Cornish mining captains had the power and influence to keep other immigrants from working their way into the mining hierarchy. The Irish, who arrived in the Copper Country in the early days of mining, also spoke English but did not have the same mining expertise as the Cornish. Religious differences between the Catholic Irish and the Methodist Cornish resulted in violent clashes between these two Celtic peoples. One of the earliest and most violent confrontations took place in Rockland on Easter Sunday, 1857, when Irish and Cornishmen attacked each other with axes and buildings were looted and burned.[30]

Although some writers thought that violence between the Cornish and the Irish was endemic, and hostility with other ethnic groups common, the opposite was actually the case. While traditional prejudice lingered, children in the mining communities attended school and mingled with a variety of youngsters, and Old Country prejudices declined as these youngsters interacted with each other. Eventually, although parental consent may have been questionable, Catholics and Methodists intermarried.[31]

Cornish Dialect and Its Influences

The Celtic languages are split into two groups: Cornish, Welsh, and Breton form one group with common roots, while Irish, Manx, and Scots Gaelic form a second group. The Cornish language was developed by a tribe called the Dumnonii who inhabited most of southwestern Britain. Here, around 2000 B.C., Cornish began to evolve as a separate language. An independent Cornish language continued in use until the eleventh century, when English became the language needed to succeed. Eventually Cornish came to be looked upon as the language of the poor people. The church acted as a further stimulus for adoption of the English language, as the Prayer Book was published only in English. Legend has it that the last Cornish speaker, Dorothy Pentreath, died in 1777 near Mousehole, although another story says that the last native Cornish speaker died around 1891 near St. Just in Penwith.

The Cornish people who came to Michigan spoke a dialect that was highly pronounced and differed from other English dialects. One of the distinctive elements of the dialect was that the Cornish pronounced the "h" when it was not necessary before vowels in words like h'apple and h'oranges, but dropped it when the it should have been in place, as in 'ome, 'otel, and 'eart.

Besides their dialect the Cornish also brought with them mining terms that were mostly Old English words given a particular meaning. There were several hundred of these, many of which were in common usage. A few of these words are as follows:

- a brave keenly lode: a fine lode of ore
- bal: mine
- deads: waste rock
- grass captain: a surface boss
- lode: a vein of ore (the term is probably derived from the verb *to lead*)
- skep or skip: the bucket-like receptacle in which ore is hoisted to the surface

- sump: the place where water is collected in the mine
- whim: the capstan used in raising ore for smaller operations

Other common terms used by Cornish people included: "to touch a pipe," meaning to smoke; "a plod," meaning a tale or story; "a passel of people," meaning a lot of people; and "tuckered out," meaning exhausted.

Cornish surnames follow prescribed forms. An old rhyme helps to explain this:

> By Tre, Ros, Car, Pol and Pen
> You may know all Cornishmen.

To best explain the prefixes: Tre means house, Ros means a heath, Car means a camp, Pol means a pool, and Pen refers to a headland.

Religious Customs

Christmas and Good Friday were the two most significant religious events on the Cornish calendar. When they settled in the Copper Country, Cornishmen spent the days before Christmas singing from house to house. Some people complained when some of them sang for ale, but this tradition continued for many years. At boardinghouses, Cornish women saw to it that Cornish boarders had access to an organ to sing and reminisce about Christmases past.[32] Some of these men were so poor that all they remembered about Christmas were the hymns, as presents were never feasible. For some, like Jim Collins, who grew up in extreme poverty, Christmas was like another Sabbath. However, in the United States, where immigrants sought to hold onto their traditions, men like Collins saw Christmas as a special time of holiday cheer to spend with family and friends. In Highland Park in the 1920s, with the influx of many new immigrants, groups of Cornishmen went from house to house singing old Cornish carols, to the delight of their countrymen.

Some of the miners provided special instructions to the children of the boardinghouse keeper. "W'y dawn't Santy visit more folks 'ere? The chimbleys be small and folks lock their doors. 'E dawn't carry keys, you know," said John Spargo, a miner who was introducing the boardinghouse missus' children to Santa Claus. On another occasion, in early December a mine captain invited all of the English miners in the neighborhood to his home to sing carols to his homesick wife. About thirty men gathered and sang a couple of "currols" like "Hark! Hark!" and "Rule Britannia." Afterward the wife provided hot tea, raisin cookies, and saffron bread as well as seedy cake and a side of scalded cream.

In the Ishpeming mines, Cornish miners sang Christmas carols as they were descending into the shaft. Once they reached the "plat" (working place), they were joined by the mining captains. The group spent a half hour singing carols before starting work. In 1920 Charles Miron introduced a more organized underground Christmas celebration. A tree was brought down and carols sung. By the 1940s the music was directed by the Ishpeming high school music teacher, and "Genial Jim" Fowler, timber boss, dressed as Santa Claus and distributed gifts. Occasionally this celebration was broadcast via the local radio station. Groups of Cornish miners also sometimes broke into carols while having drinks in the local saloon, much to surprise and amazement of out-of-town visitors.

Cornish miners and their families observed the Christmas holiday for three days: Christmas Eve, Christmas Day, and the third day, Boxing Day, when they opened their presents.

Good Friday was also an important day on the Cornish calendar. Women usually served their families fish; salted cod was common. In the Upper Peninsula the local Methodist church, under the auspices of the Sons and Daughters of St. George, would have a grand banquet and entertainment that raised funds for the church. This activity raised eyebrows among other religious adherents.

Music

The Cornish people loved music. Fine choral singing was a staple in Methodist chapels, and John Wesley encouraged his followers to "sing lustily." This tradition was brought to Michigan and the Cornish became famous for their singing and especially for their traditional songs and Christmas carols. Miners sang while walking to work and broke into a chorus as the man car took them to work in the lower levels. Rich natural baritone voices resonated on the bluffs around Central Mine. Pallbearers were heard singing "Nearer My

Good to Thee" as they carried the coffin. Copper Country choruses regularly competed to determine which was the best singing group.

In the mining communities, Cornish musicians either developed their own bands or joined city bands. The Sons of St. George lodges in Negaunee had the English Oak Band, which was a large cornet band, and Champion had the English Holly Band. These bands entered competitions and played at Cornish and non-Cornish events. When the English Oak band was disbanded, its members joined the Negaunee City band. The local bands throughout the Upper Peninsula were staffed principally by Cornish musicians.

Education

From the early days of Cornish settlement in Michigan, both immigrants and their children became involved with education. In the late nineteenth century William Bath became a county school commissioner, and others filled similar positions in other school systems. Alfred Nicholls was a notable example of persistence. After sustaining a mining injury he attended Michigan State Normal School through the financial resources provided by local fraternal organizations and the patience of his family. He served as a schoolteacher and principal at Central Mine from 1890 to 1895 and went on to become superintendent of schools in Osceola Township from 1895 to 1925.[33]

Soon after the establishment of Michigan Technological University in 1885, Cornish-American men entered the institution and graduated with mining engineer degrees. They found positions locally and around the world. Cornish-American names are found on the rolls of other Michigan colleges and universities beginning in the nineteenth century. Many Cornish-American women became teachers and principals in schools throughout Michigan. A number of Cornish immigrants, like William Hosking, found staff employment at Michigan Technological University and other colleges.

William E. Trebilcock was superintendent of Calumet Public Schools in 1936. He had worked his way up through the ranks, moving from Lake Linden High School to Ishpeming, and finally back to Calumet. Paul G. Liddicoat (1920–2001) started his professional career as a band director. Later he became a superintendent of schools in Michigan, and retired in 1982 from Wayne State University and the University of Michigan as executive director emeritus of the Metropolitan Bureau of School Studies. Others, like Scott

Holman of Northern Michigan University's Board of Trustees, served on similar boards throughout the state.

Literature and Folklore

The hardworking Cornish immigrants did not have the time or the energy to devote to the writing of their experiences in the form of autobiographies or compiled accounts. Since they were English-speaking, they did not have to develop their own newspapers as other ethnic groups did to relate their news and special stories. Local newspapers like the *Portage Lake Mining Gazette* (Houghton) and the *Marquette Mining Journal* would carry news of interest to the immigrants. From the earliest days the Upper Peninsula newspapers carried weekly columns of news from Cornwall, including prices of mine shares there, "carefully collated from [Cornish newspapers] giving the items of interest from the different towns for the benefit of our Cornish readers."[34] Besides providing news from the Old Country, the newspapers on a less formal basis provided news about Cornish residents in other parts of the United States, especially in the western mining country. Fortunately accounts of Cornish man and women can be gleaned through obituaries and sporadic stories related to these immigrants within the community.

Then there was folklore. Walter Gries (1892–1959), who lived in Ishpeming, was an educator and civic-minded citizen and affiliated with the Cleveland Cliffs Iron Company. He was a folklorist of Cornish dialect stories that were used in folklore collections, especially those of Richard Dorson. In 1946, Dorson visited the Upper Peninsula and interviewed Gries and others and preserved a substantial body of Cornish stories. These were published in his work *Bloodstoppers and Bearwalkers* in 1952.[35] Many of the tales that did not make the publication are available at the in the Dorson Papers in the Lilly Library of Indiana University–Bloomington.

The Cornish were fond of jokes, as their numerous dialect stories attest. Jokes sometimes took the form of practical jokes, which could be hard on a victim, but they were chiefly of a kindly nature. The Cornishmen are some of the few people who can enjoy jokes about their own peculiarity within their own company and never tire in telling them. "Cousin Jack" is the name given to stories of this type. A typical story follows: "A cross-eyed Cousin Jack at the Quincy [Mine] saw some large grapefruit in the window and thought they were oranges. He said, 'It wouldn't take many of they to make a dozen.' Told by James E. Fisher, Houghton, August 26, 1946."[36]

Dorson also published a series of remedies as part of Cornish traditional medicine. In 1946 he interviewed Bessie Phillips in Eagle River. In earlier years, when adults and children had sties in their eyelids, "The mother would apply a poultice of tea-leaves until the gathering would break. Another cure was passing the tail of a black cat nine times over the eyes for duble efficiency the tail should belong to a tomcat." As protection against mumps, chicken pox, and measles "all children wore around their neck a small bag of flannel containing a piece of camphor. The older folks would wear a piece of red yarn tied around their wrists or a narrow strip of red flannel wound about their waits, to help their rheumatism."[37]

Cornish immigrants and their culture and speech patterns appear in Michigan literature. Two noted authors who wrote in this venue are Cornish-born Newton G. Thomas (b. 1878) and Michigan-born John D. Voelker (1903–91).

Thomas was born in Stokes, Cornwall, and emigrated to Michigan's Upper Peninsula as a child. After growing up in these transplanted Cornish communities, he became a professor of dentistry and taught at Northwestern University Dental School, the University of Illinois, and the College of Dentistry in Chicago.

He wrote the novel *The Long Winter Ends,* which was published in 1941.[38] Using his firsthand experience, Thomas wrote about a year in the life of Jim Holman. The work looks at the trials and tribulations of this Cornish immigrant as he struggled to survive, maintain his heritage, and ultimately be assimilated into American life.

John D. Voelker was the preeminent literary figure in the Upper Peninsula, with a well-honed ability to incorporate ethnic dialects into his work. In a sense Voelker goes beyond Thomas's focus. Many of his novels and short stories incorporate Cornish and Cornish-Americans, illustrating how individuals and their culture and speech patterns were incorporated into the life and times of northern Michigan in the twentieth century.[39]

Cornish in the Wars

Cornishmen participated in all of the wars in which the United States fought, beginning with the American Revolution.[40] During the Civil War both recently arrived Cornish immigrants and Cornish-Americans and their sons served in the Union Army from Michigan. Stephen Cocking, a brigade bugler from the Upper Peninsula, served in the 23rd Michigan Volunteers. William Tresize came to the United States with his parents, who first settled in Pennsylvania and then settled permanently in the Keweenaw, and he worked in the mines until 1862. At that time he joined the 27th Michigan Volunteers and was wounded before Petersburg. Later, after returning from a mining stint in the West, Cocking became the lighthouse keeper at Copper Harbor. Cornish immigrants and Cornish-Americans have served heroically in the Spanish-American War, World War I, World War II, the Korean War, the Vietnam War, the Gulf War, and the War in Iraq.

Organizations

Cornish immigrants joined a variety of fraternal and benevolent organizations soon after their arrival in Michigan. Freemasonry lodges were established soon after the Upper Peninsula was settled, and Cornishmen became founding members of the lodges that developed. The lodge at Central Mine, a Cornish enclave, was instituted on January 8, 1868, and its membership was primarily Cornish. Cornish individuals also belonged to the Odd Fellows, the Knights of Pythias, the Temple of Honor and Temperance, and the Foresters, and later the Elks, the Eagles, the American Legion, and similar organizations.

The organization most closely associated with the Cornish people was the Order of the Sons of St. George and its women's counterpart, the Order of the Daughters of St. George.[41] The national organization, named after St. George, the patron of England, was established in Scranton, Pennsylvania, in 1871. The order rapidly spread through the coal mining regions of Pennsylvania and adjacent states and across the country. In April 1887 the English Oak Lodge No. 230 was instituted in Negaunee. The first in the state of Michigan, it was soon followed by a lodge in Ishpeming, and in rapid succession lodges were established throughout the mining communities of the western Upper

Peninsula. By 1910 there was a lodge in Detroit, and another followed in Flint.[42] Eventually there were hundreds of lodges scattered across the United States and Canada, and in 1906 membership in these lodges totaled more than thirty-five thousand. In the Upper Peninsula, the Sir Humphrey Davy Lodge in Ishpeming had the largest membership in the nation with more than three hundred names on its rolls.

While nationally this fraternal secret society was composed of Englishmen, the Upper Peninsula lodges were dominated by Cornishmen. Membership was restricted to those eighteen to fifty years of age who were eligible for sickness and death benefits. Those over fifty years of age were given honorary membership. The lodges provided newly arrived immigrants the opportunity to fraternize with fellow countrymen and assimilate into American society. Some lodges, like the English Oak of Negaunee and the English Holly of Champion, had their own bands, and others were large enough to invest in their own halls, which became revenue producers.

Besides holding frequent meetings, the society annually celebrated three important events: Good Friday, St. George's Day (April 23), and the annual summer reunion. On Good Friday the order had a popular dinner and entertainment, usually at the local Methodist church. On St. George's Day and during the summer reunion, held for several days in July or August, lodge members traveled from afar and attended parades, business meetings, speeches, musical entertainment, Cornish wrestling matches, bicycle races, and band contests. The reunions allowed immigrants from throughout the region to visit friends and relatives. The order declined in the 1930s and is no longer in existence.

The Cornish in the Lower Peninsula

Lower Michigan and the Cornish in the Twentieth Century

Hundreds of Cornish people were attracted to the Lower Peninsula in the early twentieth century as Michigan developed its urban-industrial centers. There were a number of Cornish folks at Saginaw in 1903. The women worked as nurses and teachers while the men worked in the lumber industry as managers, cutters, and millwrights; others were bricklayers, clerks, janitors, machinists, and common laborers. Edwin G. Chenoweth was a draughtsman with the Pere Marquette Railroad. Bert B. Rowe was a physician. By 1909 many Cornishmen had found jobs in Jackson and Muskegon. The Harris and Moyle families had lived in the Upper Peninsula and engaged in mining, but migrated to the Lower Peninsula in 1911. The Harris men went into the paper mills in the Kalamazoo area and then to the eastern part of the state, where they became employed in industrial jobs.[43] Grand Rapids attracted many Cornishmen, while others found jobs in the Oldsmobile plant in Lansing and still others settled elsewhere and found positions in auto and related companies.

The automobile industry developed rapidly in the opening decade of the twentieth century and needed thousands of workers. The infamous copper strike (1913–14) centered in the Copper Country brought with it suspicion, violence, and uncertainty. When Henry Ford announced in January 1914 that his workers would receive $5.00 per day, it was only natural that Cornish miners from Upper Michigan would follow their fellows southward to new opportunities in Detroit, Lansing, Flint, and other cities.

Detroit attracted not only internal immigrants, but also new arrivals from Cornwall. Large numbers of Cornishmen immigrated during the first thirty years of the twentieth century. During the 1920s Cornish immigrants sailing on ships like the *Berengaria* landed at New York City. Many of them stayed at the Cornish Arms Hotel, which had been established prior to the 1920s by Sid Blake as a temporary residence for his countryfolk. Here they got organized, changed their money, and were soon on overnight trains to Detroit. Once in Detroit many Cornishmen moved to Highland Park, where they found jobs in automobile factories.

Highland Park, an independent community enclave of Detroit, had only 427 people in 1900. Thirteen years later, Henry Ford authorized the introduction of the moving assembly line at the Highland Park plant, which was the birthplace of modern mass production. The Model T was made affordable to the average American family. Ford introduced his revolutionary pay scale of $5 a day on this site in 1914. Soon hundreds and then thousands of people were attracted to Highland Park, including many immigrants. By 1920 the population skyrocketed to 46,499, and within this number were many Cornishmen who had come from the Upper Peninsula and from the Old Country. James Edward, who immigrated in January 1920, quickly found a position in the motor assembly area. Others were employed as machinists, as toolmakers, and in other skilled positions.

Many second-generation Cornish-Americans found office positions. Walter Sleep, who had a commercial education, became an auditor, and Albert Sape was hired as an efficiency manager at Ford Motor. The younger second generation found positions as machinist apprentices, and some of the women became stenographers. The Cornish laborers found jobs in the lacquer and paint manufacturing section or in the drop forge. Not all of the Cornish worked as laborers, as some used their skills and got into construction and plumbing, or worked in various other industries and businesses. The record of the 1920 census shows that the English living in Highland Park numbered 1,445, and at 11.4 percent were the largest immigrant group, aside from Canadians. In 1919 Henry Ford moved his headquarters from Highland Park to Dearborn, but the diversified plant remained.

An Assembly Line
of the
Ford Motor Company

After 1919 hundreds of Cornish folks from the Upper Peninsula migrated to Metro Detroit and Flint, where they found jobs in the booming automobile and related industries. Source: Superior View Photography.

Nineteen-year-old Kenneth Olds, who arrived in America from Cornwall in November 1929, left some interesting insights. He found some cousins living in Highland Park and he even found a few people from his hometown, Hayle, on the streets of the community. Harry Clarke, who was in Detroit at this time, noted that when he gave a party for Cornish friends, "about forty had attended Carclaze [Elementary] school." The local Methodist church had many Cornish members, which made him feel at home. The single men found housing in boarding houses or with compatriots from the Old Country. Mr. Olds was impressed with Detroit and the automobile works, though he continued on to seek his fortune in California.

Detroit had become a great magnet for the Cornish. George E. Friggens moved to Detroit in 1919 and found employment at Cadillac Motor, Burroughs Adding Machine Company, and later at various dry-cleaning plants. Other Cornishmen found a variety of positions in booming Detroit and its suburbs. John Rule, a miner in Ironwood, decided to try his luck in Detroit working at Ford Motor Company as a tool and die man. He was not happy with factory work and eventually in 1932 he heard of a cooperative farm, Saline Valley Farms. Since he enjoyed farming, he joined the organization. Beginning in 1933 he began working in the poultry department of the Farm, then took care of the grounds and finally worked in the reception area until his retirement in 1969.

In 1923 and 1924, imitating Saturday evening visits on town and village squares in the Old Country, Cornishmen would meet at Cadillac Square in downtown Detroit and visit until roused by the police, who did not know what they were up to. Harry Clarke said they were probably "Irish cops."[44] At this time groups of Cornish people continued the tradition of singing old Cornish carols from house to house at Christmastime.

Many of the close-knit Cornish families, who were used to family picnics in the Old Country and then the Upper Peninsula, now went to Belle Isle and Palmer Park and continued the summer tradition. Their potluck luncheons included pasties, saffron bread and buns, "toad in the hole" (sausage in dough), and star-gazy pie. However, over the years American food gradually replaced the traditional fare.

A number of prominent professional men flourished in pre-1950 Detroit. William Pascoe was a successful portrait painter who made Detroit his home, but traveled and worked extensively in the United States and Europe until his death in 1946. His brother Edward was a progressive realtor whose firm helped develop the area east of downtown Detroit. Richard, one of Edward's sons, wrote Edwardian ditties for the famous Iris tenor John McCormick. Finally, there was H. J. Maxwell Grylls, who was born in Cornwall in 1865 and came to the United States in 1881. In 1907 he joined the architectural firm that dated from 1853 and became known as Smith, Hinchman and Grylls. The firm is noted for winning the competition for designing the County Hall. It also oversaw the construction of the forty-seven-story Penobscot Building, the tallest building in Detroit and the fifth-highest in the world when it was completed in 1928. The firm completed the block square J. L. Hudson department store a year later. Longtime resident of Detroit and noted American architect of the World Trade Center, Minoru Yamaski, worked with them as a young man. Today the firm has gained a national and international reputation and is known as SmithGroup.[45]

A British-American Picnic held at Palmer Park, Detroit, on July 26, 1924, was attended by this group of Cornish folks from Ironwood, who had moved south to work in the auto industry. Source: Doris Bable.

Cornish in Flint

Englishmen were attracted to Genesee County, where they numbered 1,228 in 1870, a number that remained rather constant in subsequent years. A survey of Cornish names shows no traditional names appearing in 1905. However, five years later Cornish names begin to appear in the directories as machinists, stock keepers, carpenters, and clerks.[46] In 1915 more Cornishmen were employed in metal technical positions, and in 1920 the number of Englishmen in Flint grew to 1,573, with another 399 living in Genesee County. In the years that followed Cornishmen were employed at the Armstrong Spring Company, Fisher Body Plant, Buick Motor Company, and Grand Trunk Railway. However, the majority of Cornish workers were employed by the automobile industry. By 1922 on Flint's "Old East Side" on the east bank of the Flint River there was a large community of Cornish and others who had migrated from the Copper Country. The Cornish lived in the vicinity of Asbury Methodist Church and maintained their traditions surrounding the family. The men walked across the Flint River to their jobs at the Buick Motor Company.[47]

Not everyone worked in the hustle and bustle of the automobile plant. Some Cornishmen worked in the fresh air. Fred Trevillian was a cement

H. J. Maxwell Grylls was born in Cornwall. He became an important architect and after 1907 was vice president of the firm Smith, Hinchman & Grylls, architects and engineers. He was a member of numerous Michigan architectural organizations.

contractor; Richard Tremayne, a landscape gardener; and Oscar Pascoe, a farmer. Cornish-American women were employed as teachers and principals, while others held other positions. For example, Minnie Pascoe was a saleswomen at Home Dairy, widow Dorothy Trevarthen worked in credit at Flint Oakland-Pontiac, and May Trevarrow was a factory worker.[48]

A prominent Cornish-Canadian who settled in Flint was Reverend J. Bradford Pengelly, rector of St. Paul's Episcopal Church. At first he kept to his clerical calling and was a lecturer. In the spring of 1920 he gave a series of thought-provoking public lectures on world affairs. During the decade that followed and through the mid-1930s, Pengelly operated out of the Pengelly Building in downtown Flint as the president-treasurer of the Pengelly Realty Corporation.[49]

The Depression years were hard on the people of the Upper Peninsula. The mines had been an important source of tax revenue, but when they closed because of the Depression, they no longer provided the county with funding. People who had lost their jobs found the county impoverished and unable to help them. Many Cornish people sought relief in the Lower Peninsula. Ernie Orchard, who was a youngster in Kearsarge during this time, recalled, "I often heard it said that if you were a member of the Odd Fellows and you were going to Flint or Highland Park, go to the lodge and someone might help you find a job." In the years prior to World War II it was the consensus in the Upper Peninsula that once you graduated high school, you had to leave the area for a job. Young Cornish-Americans migrated to Chicago, Milwaukee, and especially to Metro Detroit. After the war, many veterans went to Michigan Technological University or Northern Michigan University on the GI Bill, but had to relocate to southern Michigan for employment.

This out-migration had an impact on Upper Peninsula communities, again as noted by Mr. Orchard: "Since World War II the Cornish in the Copper Country are very much in the minority, both through intermarriage and great numbers leaving. This seems very apparent when I go to the Calumet Methodist Church which is now very different than when my parents attended and is having its problems."[50]

With the coming of the world depression beginning in 1929, and again after World War II, Cornish immigration fell off. In the 1930s conditions were as bad in Britain as in the United States. After the war, social legislation in Britain gave Cornishmen less incentive to emigrate.[51] Since that time there has been little emigration from Cornwall.

As urban conditions changed Cornish people migrated to the suburbs. In the early twenty-first century, their descendants are found throughout Metro Detroit cities and suburbs. A large number of Cornish-Americans reside in Flint and surrounding Genesee County; in suburban communities like Southfield, Troy, Farmington Hills, Rochester Hills, and Pontiac in Oakland County; and in Warren, Sterling Heights, and Eastpointe in Macomb County. In Wayne County Cornish-Americans are found in Redford, Livonia, Dearborn, and Dearborn Heights. Across southern Michigan descendants of the Cornish pioneers can also be found in Ann Arbor and surrounding Washtenaw County, in Lansing, in the city and suburbs of Kalamazoo, and in Grand Rapids to the north. This is only a partial listing of the communities in which Cornish-Americans live and should not be considered definitive.

The Cornish Today

The Continuing Role of Cornish Communities in the Upper Peninsula

For a relatively small ethnic group, the Cornish have developed and maintained extremely strong organizations to preserve their culture and heritage. Many descendants of Cornish immigrants maintain ties with Cornwall. A variety of cultural-heritage societies have developed over the years and are flourishing. While many larger ethnic groups see their cultural ties and organizations declining through intermarriage and a lack of interest, this is not true of Cornish-Americans. Alfred Nicholls developed the Cornish reunion for former residents of Central Mine in the Copper Country. The first reunion was held in 1907, and reunions continue to the present day. Once a time for former residents to visit and reminisce, the reunions are now attended by fourth and fifth generations from throughout the region seeking a connection to their heritage. By 1915 the remaining Cornishfolk in the Copper Country maintained good relations with their compatriots in places like Grass Valley, California, and Butte, Montana, and this tradition continued with other communities in Michigan and surrounding states.

A number of institutions have been organized to arrange reunions. Dorothy Sweet and Paul Liddicoat founded the Cornish American Heritage Society in 1982. Liddicoat was its first president. Although it started mainly as a genealogical organization, over the years it has grown to include more than five hundred members and has expanded its focus to many aspects of Cornish heritage and culture. It is affiliated with many Cornish organizations that have developed in southwestern Wisconsin, the Upper Peninsula of Michigan, California, British Columbia, and Butte, Montana. Affiliated organizations in Michigan include Cornish Connection of Lower Michigan and Keweenaw Kernewek—Cornish Connection of the Copper Country.

The first "Gathering of Cornish Cousins" was held in suburban Detroit at Fenton in 1982, and the event continues to be held on a biennial basis at locations with strong Cornish ties. Since 1993 the society has maintained a library of more than four hundred books, pamphlets, journals, and journal articles.

Individual Cornish-Americans maintain their heritage in a variety of ways. Some make and consume pasties on a weekly basis and bake saffron buns. Some Lower Peninsula Cornish groups gather for a pasty luncheon around March 5, the feast day of St. Piran, Cornwall's and the tin miners' patron saint. Others visit Cornwall frequently and belong to Cornish groups like the Cornwall Family History Society, headquartered in Truro, Cornwall, or subscribe to *Cornish World*.

The Cornish have had an important impact on Michigan. The early arrivals played essential roles in the development of mines and quarries. As the mines declined in economic importance the Cornish migrated from the Upper Peninsula to southern Michigan, where they found a variety of positions in the automobile industry. They also strengthened the presence of the Methodist church in many areas of the state, where they played important roles in the temperance movement. Throughout the years Cornish people have played a variety of roles in community service and government. At the opening of the twenty-first century, Candice Miller, of the United States House of Representatives, and the former city clerk of Marquette, Norm Gruber Jr., are both of Cornish background. The president and CEO of Bay Cast in Bay City, Scott L. Holman, was a member of the Northern Michigan University Board of Trustees. The director of the Michigan Iron Industry Museum in Negaunee, Tom Friggens, indirectly continues his family's attachment to mining, while the former director of the National Ski Hall of Fame was Ray Leverton.

The pasty has become an important part of the culinary lore of the Upper Peninsula, and saffron buns can be found in many shops throughout the region. While cricket never became a popular sport, Cornish wrestling evolved into mainstream U.S. wrestling. While this small group of immigrants is little-known to many Americans, the Cornish and their proud heritage have left an indelible mark on the development of Michigan.

Chronology of the Cornish in Michigan

1500s	Cornishmen sail with a variety of explorers to North America. Usually Cornwall is the first place the returning ships land because of the extension of Cornwall into the Atlantic Ocean.
1600s	Cornishmen continue to sail with explorers. Many begin to sail to and settle in New England where they engage in fishing and farming. As long as the Cornishmen pay their taxes, the Puritans leave them alone. These people will be the basis for many early Cornish people who settle in lower Michigan beginning in the 1830s.
1830s	Large numbers of Cornish-Americans and newly arrived immigrants are settling in Macomb, Washtenaw, Lenawee, and Oakland counties.
1843	Job and Jane Masters, early Cornish settlers, are living in Copper Harbor.
1844	Cornish miners working for the Lake Superior Mining Company sink four shafts at Eagle River.
1845	Cornish miners in the Copper Country write the *London Miners' Journal* concerning the fine copper prospects in the area.

63

1845	Newspaper editor Horace Greeley visits Eagle Harbor and notes that "Cousin Jacks" are living there and at Cliff Mine.
1846–1847	During the winter at Eagle Harbor, a Cornish Methodist congregation organizes.
1854	One of the important Cornish towns, Central Mine, in Keweenaw County is settled.
1856	Thomas A. Trevethan is engaged in mining and foundation construction at mill sites; later he is placed in charge of the Huron stamp mill and later becomes a leading merchant in Houghton.
1857	On Easter holiday a violent clash takes place in Rockland between the Irish and the Cornish.
1858	The game of cricket is introduced to Michigan in Detroit with the establishment of the Peninsula Cricket Club.
1860	Richard Trevidick goes to Saginaw and works as a head sawyer at a number of mills. Later he purchases a sawmill.
1861–1865	Numerous Cornishmen serve in the Union Army during the Civil War.
1863	A number of Cornish miners from Clifton, Keweenaw County are "going below" to the Lower Peninsula to seek their fortunes.
1863–1864	School teacher Henry Hobart writes of Cornish pioneer life at Central Mine.
1865	In Detroit, Richard F. Trevellick is president of the Shipcarpenters' and Caulkers' Local #4.
1868	A Masonic lodge is established at Central Mine where most of the members are of Cornish origin (January 8).
1869	The Central Mine Methodist Episcopal church opens and will be active until 1903.
1871	Henry Trevidick settles in Clare, becomes a merchant and serves as township treasurer and school assessor.
1871	The Order Sons of St. George is established in Scranton, Pennsylvania, and although it is founded by Englishmen it will attract many Cornish members in the Upper Peninsula.

1872	Thomas B. Dunstan is admitted to the bar in Keweenaw County, having received a law degree from the University of Michigan.
1873	Captain William Harris is elected to the state legislature to represent Ontonagon County.
1874	With the sinking of underground shafts, Cornish migration to the Marquette Range begins in earnest.
1879	James Tredenick is settled on a moderate-sized farm in Ionia County.
1879	The iron mines at Iron Mountain open and attract Cornish miners.
ca. 1880	Thomas Trewarthon, James Vial, and William Williams operate farms in Chassell, Portage, and Schoolcraft townships.
1884	When the Gogebic Range opens, the first miners are Cornishmen.
1884	Ella Mae Penglase is one of the first teachers in the Iron Mountain schools.
1885	After the establishment of Michigan Technological University, numerous Cornish-American males attend the University to become mining engineers.
1887	The "English" (Cornish in reality) of Ishpeming are sending large amounts of money to family in Cornwall.
1887	The English Oak Lodge of the Sons of St. George is established in Negaunee, the first in Michigan (April).
1888	Miner turned farmer, Thomas Trevethan, after a long career in local politics, is one of the organizers of Chassell Township.
1890	Many Cornish miners have left the Marquette Range for other mining centers.
1893	Labor strikes drive many Cornish miners to other mining centers in the Far West.
1895	A strike on the Marquette Range drives many Cornishmen to mines in Montana, Colorado, and Nevada.

1895	Cornishmen can be found as engineers, drill boys, teamsters, masons, oilers, machinists, miners, bosses, copper washers, and copper dressers.
1895	Saginaw coal mines begin to develop and attract some Cornish miners.
1895–1925	Alfred Nichols is superintendent of schools in Osceola Township, Houghton County.
1896	Thomas A. Dunstan is elected by a large majority as lieutenant governor of the state of Michigan.
1897	Emigration from Cornwall begins to decline.
1898	A mining report shows that Cornishmen comprise 25 percent of the employees on the Marquette Range.
1899	In Detroit Samuel M. Trevellich is an attorney, Trebilock & Bros are jewelers, and Philip H. Resize is a real estate agent.
1905	James and William Tonkin migrate to Austin, Nevada, to mine sliver.
1906	With more than three hundred members, the Sir Humphrey Lodge (Sons of St. George) has the largest membership in the United States.
1907	H. M. Maxwell Grylls joins the architectural firm which will become known as Smith, Hinchman and Grylls. They will work on many famous buildings in Detroit.
1908	William R. Oates, born in Cornwall, is elected on the Republican ticket and goes on to serve several terms in the state legislature representing the Copper Country.
1909	Jack Carkeek of Michigamme has a national reputation in Cornish and other forms of wrestling.
1911	The Moyle family leaves the mines of the Upper Peninsula and settles on a farm in Mattawan, west of Kalamazoo.
ca. 1912	Cornishmen are working in Kalamazoo paper mills.
1913	Thomas Buzzo's family is scattered across the U.S. and found in the Minnesota iron ranges, Butte, Salt Lake City, Chicago, Ishpeming, and British Columbia.
1913–1914	During the infamous copper strike, Cornishmen are found on both sides of the strike.

1916	The Ahmeek Athletic Association holds some of the most successful Cornish wrestling tournaments in the Copper Country.
1918	Ella Penglase retires from teaching and joins her sister Jenny M. Penglase to operate the Penglase Business College in Iron Mountain until 1946.
1919	Many Cornish people leave the Upper Peninsula for the booming automobile job market in Metro Detroit.
1923	There is an unsuccessful attempt at reviving cricket in the Copper Country.
1920s	Cornish women in Detroit are sales ladies at Kern's Department Store, stenographers with the public library, fitters for Crowley Sisters Corset Shop, and dental assistants.
1920s	There are so many Cornish immigrants in Highland Park they are able to revive singing Christmas carols going from house to house.
1920s	Cornish families hold picnics at Belle Isle Park and Palmer Park in Detroit.
1920	Charles Miron introduces the underground Christmas celebration in Ishpeming, which most Cornish miners take part in over the years.
1922	On Flint's "Old East Side" on the east bank of the Flint River there is a large community of Cornishmen and others who migrated from the Copper Country; many work at the Buick Motor Company.
1923	Many Cornish immigrants meet at Cadillac Square in Detroit to visit as they did in the old country.
1928	Smith, Hinchman, and Grylls design and oversee the construction of the forty-seven story Penobscot Building, the then-tallest building in Detroit and the fifth tallest in the world.
1929	Cornishmen in Flint are working as cement contractors, landscape gardeners, and farmers; the women are employed as teachers, saleswomen, and factory workers.

1930s	In the Copper Country many second generation Cornish people have left the mines and have found employment in non-mining fields.
1932	John Rule, a former miner from Ironwood, has been employed with Ford Motor Company and eventually gets a job as a poultry man at a farm co-operative in Saline Valley.
1935	Episcopal priest and realtor J. Bradford Pengelly operates out of the Pengelly Building in downtown Flint as president-treasurer of the Pengelly Realty Corporation.
1941	Newton G. Thomas, a Cornish immigrant, publishes *The Long Winter Ends,* a novel about Cornish life in the Upper Peninsula.
1946	Folklorist Richard M. Dorson collects many Cornish folktales from throughout the Upper Peninsula.
1946	With the passing of William Pascoe the Detroit community loses a successful portrait painter.
1947	Many Cornish-American veterans use the GI Bill to attend Michigan Technological University and Northern Michigan University but settle in the Lower Peninsula where jobs are available.
1952	Dorson publishes some of his Cornish folktales in *Blood-Stoppers and Bear Walkers: Folk Traditions of the Upper Peninsula.*
1982	Dorothy Sweet and Paul Liddicoat found the Cornish American Heritage Society.
1982	The first "Gathering of Cornish Cousins" is held in suburban Detroit at Fenton.
1992	Candice Miller, descendant of Cornish immigrants, is elected as secretary of state of Michigan.
2002	Miller wins a seat in the U.S. House of Representatives.
2005	Thousands of Cornish-Americans reside in northern Metro Detroit.
2007	Hundreds of Cornish-Americans continue to return in late July to Central Mine, on the Keweenaw Peninsula, to celebrate their religious and cultural heritage.

Cornish Life in Ishpeming, Michigan

by Sarah Bottrell (b. 1904; interviewed 2005)

Sarah Bottrell provides interesting insights into life in a Cornish family in the Michigan mining town of Ishpeming. Sarah attended Northern Michigan University where she got a life-teaching certificate and went on to teach History and Social Studies in Newberry and Marquette until her retirement in 1970.

My father, Richard Bottrell was a miner. He hadn't been in Europe. He was a fisherman on the Atlantic. That's strange you know you come to a new world and a new life. How could he stand being out in the ocean and then working in an underground mine? You do what the economics is around you, yeh?

He was from Cornwall, in England. The closest important town is Penzance. They were from a fishing village called Redruth. I think he left the old country because the relatives had died. My mother, Catherine (Jones) had one brother who came to Lake Linden. I don't know whether that attracted them. I know when they came to the United States they went to Lake Linden first. They did not like it there at all. My father came down to Ishpeming just on a lark, you might say, with no job. They had twin boys (Harry and Thomas), two and a half years old. But they made it. He went from fishing to mining, it doesn't make any sense. It was a job, food for the family. It is all that you can call it, you know.

At home we ate pasties and saffron cake. The other day there was a little box in the mail box. This was strange as I hadn't sent for anything. And it was a saffron cake from my friend in Penzance. It was from a famous baker, Warner's Bakery in the town of St. Just. We get something like it here, but it isn't quite the same thing you know. They make it so rich it is really like cake and full of currants. I've never had that before. So there is my birthday present. It came 4,000 miles!

What was life like in Ishpeming for a Cornish family? The miners got $2.50 a day for ten months. And that's what you lived on. I must have had it easy because I never went without nice clothes and had plenty of food all the time. I don't have any bad memories. I must have had a good mother, who did all those things for us.

We did not keep chickens or a garden because we lived right in the middle of town. I was surprised at reading some of those statistics. The population of Ishpeming was 10,000. See I grew up in a city and knew city life. I didn't know anything about agricultural life. At that time there were ninety-two different mines in the general area extending to Gwinn, Palmer, and so forth.

My father thought mining was hard work. He became sort of a dynamite specialist you might say, which is a pretty important job in the mine. Some years ago out on West Bluff [in Ishpeming] those houses are on rock. The city was doing some building there at that time. They asked my father if he would do some of the dynamiting. He refused this job although he was clever at it in the mine.

They worked in partners. They had morning, afternoon and night shifts that they had to keep alternating. This particular day, my father was afternoon shift and so he put in his time and came home. His partner, a Swedish man called Mr. Carlson went into the same raise for night shift. It caved in and killed him. My father should have been on that shift. I would have been a little girl in poverty. Let me tell you because there was one man whom they called the poor commissioner. I guess he was elected and he was a toughie. I know our neighbor's husband died and she had three children and he allotted her $10 a month to live on. So I was lucky, I had my father who always worked.

I have to tell this family joke on him. The miners would get some of the red dust of the iron ore in their ears. He must have had it and he got sort of deaf, so we were led to believe. We at home, had to be hollering so he could hear us. Well, this one morning my mother and he were at breakfast before he left for work. My mother said in a near-whisper, "Are you going to work this morning?" Suddenly he answers, "What makes you think I am not going to work, don't I always go to work? She whispered to him and he heard it. This was a family joke for years.

We had pasties every now and then. We never had them on a special day as some Cornish families did. There was one thing that we always had. For one thing we had coffee once a week, on Sunday morning. That was a treat because we usually had tea, being English. On Sunday mornings we had cod fish and coffee, a special Sunday morning breakfast. The salted and dried cod fish, a great plank fish, was soaked in water for a day or two to get all of the intense salt out of it. Then it was boiled. It had a white sauce poured over it which the Cousin Jacks called "dippy." It wasn't completely white sauce; it had this special Colman's mustard powder in it. It was like golden. We poured the sauce over the cod fish. It's like you use white sauce on salmon or whatever. You also had bread and butter with the cod and dippy. We did not have it with potatoes in Sunday morning. If we had cod and dippy for a regular meal we would have it with potatoes and a vegetable.

In high school I always wanted to be a teacher. There was no problem to it. I just came from high school to Northern State Normal School, which is now Northern Michigan University. My parents moved the dozen miles to Marquette so that I would be closer to school. I continue to live in the family home a mere block from the campus where I attended classes over eighty years ago.

Growing Up in a Cornish Household: Food

by George Holman (b. 1911; interviewed 2004)

Well, mother Carrie made pasties when I was a young boy, every Saturday. That was our Saturday meal and in the summer time we could take it out in the yard or out in the woods wherever we lived. The pasty was a unit in itself. It had a crust on it, and the favorite pasty of mine was meat and potatoes and lots of onions. And I remember mother sitting or standing over the table with her apron on, concocting these delicious pasties—they were the food of the gods. And we always loved Saturdays because it was pasty day, and her pasties were famous as far as us kids were concerned, because she did a wonderful job with pasty making, and had them often enough so that it was a part of our life. My meat and bones are mostly pasties.

I remember when I was old enough, carrying a pasty on Saturday to my dad who was working in a Negaunee mine, called the Athens Mine. Mother would make the pasties in the morning and wrap them in newspaper. Stan and I would take three pasties with us. One for dad who would come up from the mine to eat on the surface with us and we would sit on the bench and talk. Stan and I would eat our pasties and dad would eat his. It was just a wonderful part of our growing up.

We still have pasties. My wife was a Swede, whose mother made pasties, adapted from the English pasty, and she made the recipe very much like the one Carrie used to make. And in fact about a week ago I took one out of the freezer and warmed it up, and it was one of the traditional pasties.

Mother Carrie made them by making up the dough which was not as rich as pie crust but it held together. She would put a dinner plate on the flattened dough and trace a knife around the plate and that was the size of the pasty which was a pretty good pasty. And we still make them very much the same way.

It was a two-handed pasty. If we were sitting at the table, we would most often cut it in half and eat one half first, and we always finished the pasty. When I was a little boy, mother would make smaller pasties to take on picnics. I remember one time, believe it or not, when I was a growing boy probably 14-15 years old, when I could eat four or five of those picnic pasties at once. And I was teased a little bit because of my horrendous appetite. But the pasties were so good that you could hardly stop eating them while you had enough room in your stomach for another one.

There was one other favorite food that mother Carrie made which was brought over from England—the saffron bun. It is a very delicious bun with raisins and is the color and flavor of saffron. Saffron is very, very expensive. I don't know how much it is now, but it's more expensive than platinum per ounce. We'd buy it, and we'd make a batch of pasties. I think it cost us something in the neighborhood of twenty dollars for a little two or three ounces. Saffron goes a long ways because it comes from the stamens of a flower. Real saffron comes from Spain. The real saffron, in stores around Spokane is kept under lock and key in the safe. And I was at one of the stores here early on, like ten years ago, and I asked them if they had saffron, and the gal said, "Yeah, but you have to ask the manager." So I asked him, I said, "Where is he?," and she pointed him out, and I asked him, and he said, "Well, come with me." So he goes to the safe and gets me a little package of saffron. Evidently it was so valuable that in the city of Spokane people lifted it. Although it was expensive, it was one of those traditions that came from the English, from Cornwall, brought over by my mother Carrie, and I suppose all the other Cousin Jennies that came over.

One of my favorite foods was something that nobody else likes and my wife Evelyn never would ever make it. But when mother would come to visit us in lower Michigan, she would say, "What would you like for me to make George?" and I would say, "A kidney pie." And a kidney pie is as it says, made from kidneys. And I can still remember at our house in Ishpeming, the day that mother would make the kidney pie. You'd have to really open the doors afterward because it smelled like the product of kidneys. It was not a very good smell, but I suppose growing up with the odor, we transferred the odor into the wonderful taste of the kidney pie. I think Evelyn would always arrange a bridge club or something to get out of the house while this was going on.

Appendix 4

The Pasty on the Move

The traditional pasty, saffron cake or buns, and heavy "caker" were the common foods of the Cornish. Outside of the Chinese, the Cornish were one of the few immigrant groups whose food became a staple fare in the various centers where Cornish immigrants migrated.

The pasty is the most important and well-known food brought by the Cornish and is closely associated with mining. It provided not only food for the miners underground, but a wealth of legend and color to the Cornish story in America. Today it continues to be eaten at various locations throughout the United States. One of its problems is that although it provided a substantial meal for miners, today pasty can be considered a bit "too heavy" for some people, especially in the evening.

In the Midwest, pasty production is a cottage industry in a number of communities. As the market expands so does the production of pasties and, as a result, this process has been mechanized. Purists in the business insist that automation destroys the true pasty, its flavor, and its ethnicity, but obviously this is highly debatable.

In Michigan, the pasty is produced at many locations in both the Upper and Lower Peninsulas. From St. Ignace on the east and stretching across the Upper Peninsula to Gogebic County on the west, communities have their pasty bakeries, restaurants, and specialty shops. In the 1960s, local chambers of commerce like that in Marquette promoted the idea of making May 24 official "Pasty Day." Upper Peninsula telephone books are some of the few in the country that have "Pasties—Meat Pies" in their listings.

Newspaper stories relate one of the early pasty shops in the Upper Peninsula. Romeo Rochelaeu, owner and head baker of the Home Bakery in Iron Mountain, started in 1932 making Cornish pasties as a side line to bring in some extra money during the Great Depression. Rochelaeu, a baker of French background, commercialized the Cornish pasty. This baker is an example of how non-Cornish people enjoyed the pasty, its preparation and sale.

Rochelaeu's business went well and he had two former street transit buses converted into mobile pasty concession stands and they were used at agricultural fairs and other special events. In 1962, the Home Bakery sold 4,000 to 5,000 pasties weekly in the summer to tourists and area residents. The bakery ceased operations in the summer of 1964.

An early and well-known pasty shop in the Marquette area was Madelyne's Pasties, which opened in the 1950s and then in 1965 moved to Ishpeming. They were the first to fast freeze pasties for shipment. For years they were one of the largest producers, but they ceased production in 1981. Lawry's Pasties first opened in Ishpeming and later opened branches in Marquette and Harvey. In 1966, Roger Lawry converted forty tons of potatoes, nine tons of vegetables, four tons of lard, twelve tons of flour, and fifteen tons of strip steak into enough pasties to stretch five miles laid end to end. In the late 1980s, Nancy Lawry told the food writers Jane and Michael Stern that she started every morning making pasties from scratch and by the end of the day had produced as many as two to four hundred. One Fourth of July Lawry set a single-day record with seven hundred pasties. Beginning in the 1980s, Lawry's appeared in *Roadside Food and Good Food* by Jane and Michael Stern, which is a guide to good regional food. These gourmets were thoroughly impressed with Lawry's pasty and concluded, "You understand their popularity in the cold north woods when you take possession of a Lawry's pasty. Just to hold this big piece of food imparts a feeling of security." Although the Lawrys guard their recipe, the Sterns created one which appeared in their *Real American Food.* Today the Lawry's maintain stores in West Ishpeming and Marquette.

In Marquette there is Jean-Kay's Pasties & Subs, which produces both traditional pasties and their vegetarian variety. Pasties are on the menu of

Northern Michigan University and enjoyed by students and faculty. Small hors d'oeuvre pasties are served at receptions on campus and elsewhere. Throughout the Upper Peninsula in communities like St. Ignace, Escanaba, Iron Mountain, Rapid River, Laurium, and Ironwood pasties are available in shops and restaurants.

Just across the Wisconsin-Michigan border in Florence, Wisconsin, is home to The Pasty Oven, Inc. As of 2005 they were selling a variety of frozen pasties throughout Upper Peninsula food stores. The varieties of available pasties include: Traditional Cornish Pasty with beef and pork and another with rutabagas; Pizza Pasty with pepperoni; Vegetable Pasty; Chicken Pasty with cheese; and finally the Mini-Traditional Pasty with beef and pork. Although some of these pasty types would shock any self-respecting Cornish immigrant, they do show that pasties are made to sell, and it should be remembered that historically the Cornish made pasties of a variety of available fillings, from marine mammals to deer and even vegetables and weeds during hard times.

From the Lower Peninsula city of Flint and a center of Cornish-American migration in the 1920s, pasties are produced and sold throughout Michigan and in the Chicago area under the UP Brand. In downtown Traverse City there is Cousin Jenny's Cornish Pasties. In Redford, a Detroit suburb, Ackroyd's Scotch Bakery & Sausage sells a variety of Celtic bakery goods, including a light-crusted pasty.

The center of pasty cuisine in neighboring Wisconsin is Mineral Point in the southwestern corner of the state. Here in the former lead mining region with its strong Cornish heritage, the pasty remains king. Elsewhere in the state pasties are procured commercially, as in Menominee Falls, a suburb of Milwaukee.

The largest pasty ever recorded was made by Northern Michigan University students on October 20, 1978. They brought together 250 pounds of beef, four hundred pounds of potatoes, seventy-five pounds of carrots, and twenty-five pounds of onions, and wrapped the ingredients into 250 pounds of dough. Several hundred people enjoyed this monster pasty.

The humble pasty has entered the world of music. Kitty Donohue produced an album, *Bunyan and Banjoes: Sons of Michigan and the Great Lakes*, in 1987 and re-released it in 2004 as a favorite of many people. "Ode to the Pasty" is one of the few songs which celebrates an ethnic food from Michigan.

In the Far West, the pasty thrives in a variety of locations. In the vicinity of Butte, Montana, a copper mining center which attracted hundreds of Cornish miners in the nineteenth century, the pasty is part of the local cuisine. Shops making and selling them are common, and they appear on local restaurant menus. The biggest difference in Butte, Montana's consumption is that more than likely pasties will be served with gravy. Upper Peninsula pasty purists cringe at the mere thought of ruining a delicious pasty with gravy, while they will not hesitate to douse it with catsup—but don't tell that to the Butte purist. Entering the debate on whether or not gravy or sauce should be put on your pasty is Wheat's Treats Inc. out of the tiny village of Christmas, Michigan, some forty miles east of Marquette. Here, under the name of two Finnish-American folk heroes, they produce and ship out Toivo & Eino's Pasty Sauce. As the instructions state, the sauce can be used on pasties and on other food items as well.

Aficionados and others have spread the pasty beyond the confines of the Midwest. The pasty is now found in Florida and other locations where Michiginians are found during the winter months and in California malls. A western outpost for the pasty is Grass Valley in the California gold country, once home to hundreds of Cornish miners.

Recent investigations into the ethnic history of Mexico show that the pasty even found its way into that nation. The city of Pachuca in the state of Hidalgo, some seventy-five miles northeast of Mexico City, has a long silver-mining history. As a matter of fact, today much of Mexico's silver production comes from the vicinity of Pachuca. During the nineteenth century, Cornish miners settled in the area at Real del Monte and introduced Mexicans to soccer and the pasty. Today neighborhood restaurants in Pachuca carry pasties on their menus. Here, too, the traditional pasty has undergone a change, as these are filled with chile, meats, moles, and other Mexican-style adaptations. However, a recent Mexican cook book with a pasty recipe shows that it is made in a traditional manner as well.

Mainstream America frequently uses foodways as a factor in identifying ethnic and regional character. This is certainly true of the humble pasty. Despite its folklore and arguments over what constitutes the "best" pasty, the little meat pie is one of the local ethnic foods that has become closely associated with the Upper Peninsula and helps to give the region its special identity.

Home Remedies and Special Drinks from Cornwall

by Doris Bable

- *Colds.* Take 1 teaspoon of powdered ginger and 1 teaspoon of honey and mix in a cup of very hot water. Drink and go to bed.
- *Earache.* Mix onion juice with warmed oil and put in the ear.
- *Tea.* Drinking "lots of teas" of any variety will keep you healthy and relaxed.
- *Upset Stomach.* Place a drop of wintergreen oil in hot water and drink.
- *To Keep the Body "Balanced".* Place 1 teaspoon of vinegar and 1 tablespoon of honey in a cup of hot water or cider. Drink daily.
- *To Keep Regular.* Eat prunes or bran on a regular basis.

No measurements are given here, so you will have to improvise and mix to your taste. Drink warm or with ice.

- *Samson.* Mix brandy, cider, and sugar together.
- *Shenackerum.* This drink is made of home-brewed beer or store-bought beer, Jamaican rum, lemon, brown sugar, and nutmeg.

Appendix 6

Cornish Recipes

Plum Pudding *by Merton Holman, Negaunee, Michigan*

1 lb. / 4 cups ground suet
½ tsp. baking powder
2 eggs
2 cups raisins
2 tsp. cinnamon
1 tsp. nutmeg
2 tsp. allspice
3 cups flour

Mix with hands and at least 1 cup of milk until the mixture is firm together. Place mixture in a piece of muslin and hang in a pot of water. Boil for three hours.

Sauce

1 pint water
½ cup sugar
2 Tbsp. margarine/butter

Bring to a boil and then simmer until thickened. Remove the plum pudding from the muslin, place on a serving dish, and pour the sauce over the pudding.

Saffron Bread or Rolls *by Betty Leverton, Ishpeming, Michigan*

1 pkg. / 0.06 oz. saffron

1 cup margarine

6 cups flour

1 cup sugar

2 tsp. salt

2 cups currants

3 envelopes of dry yeast

½ cup warm water

Soak 1 package of saffron in 1 cup of hot water overnight or longer. Mix together 1 cup margarine, 6 cups of flour, 1 cup of sugar, 2 teaspoons of salt. Add 2 cups of currants that have been rinsed and drained. In a separate bowl soak 3 envelopes of dry yeast in ½ cup of warm water. Add saffron water to the dry ingredients. Add yeast mixture and mix all ingredients together. Place in a greased bowl and let rise in a warm place until doubled. Punch down and shape into loaves or rolls, placing them into baking pans. Keep in a warm place to let rise again.

Bake at 350° for 30 minutes. This recipe does not require kneading. Makes 3 loaves or about 30 rolls.

Mother Holman's Pasties *by Louisa Holman, Negaunee, Michigan*

Take a sieveful of flour, three-fourths of a cup of lard, two tablespoons of suet, and enough water to work up a smooth dough. Roll out the dough and cut six to eight potatoes into slices. Add two pounds of cubed beef (or beef and pork mixture), onion, and turnip to taste. Season thoroughly. Fold over the pasty and seal the edges by crinkling. Bake 45 minutes to an hour, depending on the fire. Wrap in oiled paper and clean dish towels, and the pasties will stay hot 8 to 9 hours.

Ethel Morcom Rule's UP Pasties (1911) *by Doris Bable, Saline, Michigan*

3 cups flour

1 cup suet, ground fine

½ cup lard

1 tsp. salt

6–7 Tbsp. cold water

1 lb. diced or cubed beef—good quality

½ lb. diced or cubed pork—good quality

"Ample" potatoes, onions, and turnips—cubed or diced

A few knobs of butter, pepper, parsley, and a bit of salt.

Combine the first ingredients: flour, suet, lard, salt, and cold water and mix. Then take the prepared meat and vegetables, mix them, and place in the middle of a circle of dough. Fold dough and crimp. Bake at 400° for one hour (wood stove temperature).

Seedy Cake *by Arlene Pearce Felt, National Mine, Michigan*

4 oz. sugar

4 oz. butter

2 eggs

4 oz. flour

1 tsp. caraway seeds

Salt pinch

Cream butter and sugar. Whisk yolks and whites of eggs separately. Gradually add flour, yolks and whites, and the caraway seeds. Bake 30 minutes to 45 minutes in an oven at 350°.

Cod and Dippy *by Sarah Bottrell, Marquette, Michigan*

Use salted cod with cream-colored fillets. Avoid the brown ones. This can either be a side of dried salted cod or cod in a little wooden box. Frozen cod can be substituted but will lack the texture of the salted cod.

Rinse the cod and then place it in a bowl of cold water to soak a day ahead. On your preferences change the water frequently. When desalted, place the cod in a pot and boil for 20 minutes. When done cut into pieces.

Dippy

2 Tbs. butter

2 Tbs. all-purpose flour

½ tsp. salt

dash pepper

1 tsp. mustard powder

1 cup milk

In a medium saucepan over a low heat melt butter. Then stir in the flour, salt, pepper, and mustard until smooth. Gradually stir in milk; cook stirring constantly, until thickened and smooth. Makes one cup.

Pour the dippy over the boiled cod which has been kept warm. For breakfast serve alone or at other meals include potatoes and vegetables.

Notes

1. Richard Carew, *The Survey of Cornwall*. (1602; New York: Da Capo Press, 1969).
2. Brian Carpenter, "Cricket in Teigmouth, 1773," *Devon and Cornwall Notes and Queries* 37, no. 7 (Spring 1995): 218–19.
3. Carew, *Survey of Cornwall*, 114–15.
4. As the years of the twentieth century progressed so did the decline in Cornish mining activity. In 1998 the South Crofty tin mine closed and brought mining to an end in Cornwall. However, there was serious talk of a revival of mining at this site.
5. For an excellent introduction to the earliest Cornish settlers to the United States, see A. L. Rowse, *The Cousin Jacks: The Cornish in America* (New York: Scribner's Sons, 1969), 3–160.
6. Tombstones in the Raisin Township cemetery list numerous Cornish names in this farming community. Many settlers here were from New York Sate.
7. *Portrait and Biographical Album of Ionia and Montcalm Counties, Michigan* (Chicago: Chapman Bros., 1891), 449–50.
8. Edith Moyle in Russell M. Magnaghi, compiler, *The Cornish in Michigan Project 2002* (Marquette: Belle Fontaine Press, 2002).
9. *Portrait and Biographical Album of Isabella County, Michigan* (Chicago: Chapman Brothers, 1884), 287–88.
10. *Lake Superior News*, 18 July 1846.

11. John Anderton, "A Cultural Resource Survey of Presque Isle," presented at the Sonderegger Symposium II, Northern Michigan University, 15 November 2002.

12. The terms "Cousin Jack" and "Cousin Jenny" are used to describe Cornish people. It refers to the time when there were so many related Cornish people in an area that they were all referred to as cousins.

13. Federal Census, Michigan, Chippewa, Michilimackinac, Marquette, Houghton, and Ontonagon counties, 1850.

14. Two studies of this community are: Clarence J. Monette, *Central Mine—A Ghost Town* (Calumet, Mich.: Greenlee Printing Company, 1995); and Keweenaw County Historical Society, compiler, *Central Mine, Years of Hard Work—Lives of Pain and Hope* (Keweenaw County Historical Society, 1998).

15. *Reports of the Immigration Commission, Immigrants in Industries.* 41 vols. (Washington, D.C.: Government Printing Office, 1911), 16:81–92.

16. *Mining Journal,* 22 April 1902.

17. *Mining Journal,* 2 August 1913.

18. Arthur W. Thurner's *Rebels on the Range: The Michigan Copper Miners Strike 1913– 1914* (Lake Linden, Mich.: John H. Forster Press, 1984) provides a fine overview of the struggle.

19. *History of the Upper Peninsula of Michigan* (Chicago: Western Historical Company, 1883), 339.

20. *Iron Mountain Press,* 28 February 1950.

21. Interview with Doris Rule Bable, Saline, Michigan, 7 March 2002, deposited at the Bentley Library, University of Michigan, Ann Arbor.

22. Arthur C. Todd, *The Cornish Miner in America* (Glendale, Calif.: Arthur Clark Company, 1967), 144–46.

23. John H. Forster, "Life in the Copper Mines of Lake Superior," *Michigan Pioneer and Historical Collection* 11 (1887):179–80.

24. Jane and Michael Stern, *Real American Food* (New York: Alfred Knopf, 1986), 236.

25. Carpenter, "Cricket in Teignmouth," 218–19.

26. *Marquette Mining Journal,* 23 July 1892, 11 July 1908, 17 April 1909, and 1 May 1909.

27. Carew, *Survey of Cornwall,* 75–76.

28. "Regular" wrestling had developed around the catch-as-catch-can and Greco Roman styles.

29. *Marquette Weekly Mining Journal,* 27 July 1907.

30. James K. Jamison, "The Copper Rush of the 50s," *Michigan History* 19 (1935): 371–90.

31. Interview with Merton, Milton, and Sidney Holman, Negaunee, Michigan, 21 December 2001, deposited at the Central Upper Peninsula and University Archives, Northern Michigan University, Marquette, Michigan.

32. Mrs. A.H. Albeiter, "How They Celebrated Christmas: The Cornish," *Wisconsin Tales and Trails* 3, no. 4 (Winter 1962): 1–4.

33. Judith Rowe Jarve, ed., "From the Journal of Alfred Nicholls, Central Mine School Teacher and Principal, 1890–1925," in *Central Mine: Years of Hard Work—Lives of Pain and Hope,* comp. Keweenaw County Historical Society, (N.p.: Keweenaw County Historical Society, 1998), 24–26.

34. *Portage Lake Mining Gazette* (Houghton), 25 June 1885; *Copper Country Evening News* (Calumet), 2 June 1914 and 26 December 1914; *Le Courrier du Michigan* (Lake Linden), June 1919.

35. Richard M. Dorson, *Bloodstoppers and Bearwalkers: Folk Traditions of the Upper Peninsula* (Cambridge, Mass.: Harvard University Press, 1952).

36. Dorson Papers, Lilly Library, Indiana University.

37. Richard Dorson, *Bloodstoppers and Bearwalkers* (Cambridge: Harvard University Press, 1952), 116–17.

38. Newton G. Thomas, *The Long Winter Ends* (New York: Macmillan, 1941; Detroit: Wayne State University Press, 1998).

39. Although many of Voelker's works incorporate the Cornish, some examples can be found in *Danny and the Boys: Being Some Legends of Hungry Hollow* (Cleveland and New York: World Publishing Company, 1951; Detroit: Wayne State University Press, 1987), 23–25, 126; *Trouble-Shooter: The Story of A Northwoods Prosecutor* (New York: Viking Press, 1943), 20, 241, 246–247; and *Laughing Whitefish* (New York: McGraw -Hill Book Company, 1965), 9–10.

40. A. L. Rowse, *The Cousin Jacks: The Cornish in America* (New York: Charles Scribner's Sons, 1969), 73–74, 140–42, 107–8, 135, 203–4.

41. For a detailed account of this organization see: Russell M. Magnaghi, *A Preliminary History of the Order, Sons of St. George in Michigan* (Marquette: Belle Fontaine Press, 2003).

42. Lodges were established in Beacon/Champion, Calumet/Red Jacket, Central Mine, Detroit, Flint, Hancock, Iron Mountain, Houghton, Iron River, Ironwood, Ishpeming, Lake Linden, Marquette, National Mine, Negaunee, Norway, Painesdale, Quincy, Republic, Trimountain, and Winthrop.

43. Edith Moyle in Magnaghi, *Cornish in Michigan Project 2002.*

44. Rowse, *Cousin Jacks,* 422.

45. Ibid., 180–81.

46. Traditional Cornish names reviewed included: Berryman, Pasco, Pemberthy, Tregilas, Treice, and Trevan.

47. Interview with Doug Wilkinson, Gwinn, Michigan, 30 April 2003, deposited at Bentley Historical Library, University of Michigan, Ann Arbor.

48. *Flint City Directory, 1929* (Detroit: R.L. Polk & Co., 1929), 160, 699, 705, 892–93.

49. *Flint Journal,* 24 April 1920.

50. Ernie Orchard in Magnaghi, *Cornish in Michigan Project 2002.*

51. Rowse, *Cousin Jacks,* 420.

For Further Reference

Archives and Libraries

Bentley Historical Library, University of Michigan, 1150 Beal Ave., Ann Arbor, Mich. 48109-3482; 734/764-3482; fax 734/936-1333; *www.umich.edu/-bhl/*. Resources: interviews, newspaper clippings, photographs, and notes for this study.

Burton Historical Collection, Detroit Public Library, 5201 Woodward Ave., Detroit, Mich. 48202; 313/833-1486; *http://www.detroit.lib.mi.us/burton/index.htm* Resources: newspaper clippings, photographs, and obituaries.

Central Upper Peninsula and University Archives, Northern Michigan University, 1401 Presque Isle Avenue, Marquette, Mich. 49855; 906/227-1225; *http://www .nmu. edu/olsonlibrary/archives/index.htm*; e-mail: *mrobyns@nmu.edu* Resources: oral interviews and paper materials.

Cornish-American Connection, The Secretary, Murdoch House Adult Education Centre, Cross Street, Redruth, Cornwall TR15 2BU; 01209 2163333. Resources: genealogical and related information.

Cornish Language Advisory Service, *http://www.clas.demo.co.uk*. Resources: promotes all of the traditional forms of the Cornish language.

Cornwall Family History Society, 5 Victoria Square, Truro, Cornwall, TR1 2RS UK; +44 1872 264044; *http://www.cornwallfhs.com*. Resources: materials and researchers to assist members in tracing their family history.

Institute of Cornish Studies, University of Exeter; *http://www.ex.ac.uk/~cnfrench/ics/*
Iron County Historical Museum, Museum Road, P.O. Box 272, Caspian, Mich. 49915;
906/265-2617; *www.iron/museum.com/* Resources: clippings, photographs,
paper materials, and artifacts.

John H. Longyear Library, Marquette County Historical Society, 213 N. Front Street,
Marquette, Mich. 49855; 906/266-3571. Resources: photographs, paper materials, and artifacts.

Library of Michigan, 717 W. Allegan Street, P.O. Box 30007, Lansing, Mich. 48909-7507;
517/373-1580. Resources: variety of genealogical materials, census reports, city
directories, and newspapers.

Lilly Library, Indiana University, Bloomington, Ind. 47405-33011; 812/855-2452; fax
812/855-3143; e-mail: *liblilly&indiana.edu*; Homepage: *http://www.indiana.edu/
~lilly/* Resources: the Richard Dorson Papers, which contain folkloric interviews
with Cornish immigrants in the Upper Peninsula conducted in 1946.

Menominee Range Historical Association, 300 E. Ludington Street, Iron Mountain,
Mich. 49801-4276. Resources: artifacts, photographs, and paper materials.

Michigan Technological University Archives and Copper Country Historical Collections, J. Robert Van Pelt Library, 1400 Townsend Drive, Houghton, Mich. 49931;
906/487-2505; e-mail: *copper@mtu.edu* Resources: employee records, paper materials, newspapers, and photographs.

Superior View Studios, 156 W. Washington Street, Marquette, Mich. 49855; 906/225-
1952. Resources: extensive photographic collection of the Upper Peninsula.

Published Sources

Albeiter, Mrs. A. H. "How They Celebrated Christmas: The Cornish," *Wisconsin Tales
and Trails* 3, no. 4 (Winter 1962): 1–4.

Anderson, James M., and Iva A. Smith, eds. *Ethnic Groups in Michigan*. Vol. 2, *The
Peoples of Michigan*. Detroit: Ethnos Press, 1983.

Anderton, John. "A Cultural Resource Survey of Presque Isle." Paper presented at the
Sonderegger Symposium II, Northern Michigan University, 15 November 2002.

Berthoff, Rowland. *British Immigrants in Industrial America*. Cambridge: Harvard
University Press, 1953.

Browne, Mary Jo Russell. "A Comparative Study between the Miner's Homes in Cornwall and the Miner's Home of the Cornish in Michigan." Master's thesis, University of Minnesota, 1986.

Buckley, J. A. *The Cornish Mining Industry: A Brief History.* Redruth, Cornwall: Tor Mark Press, 1988.

Buell, Robert R. *Cornish Records of Northern Michigan Copper Mines: Remittances to Cornwall 1876.* Ann Arbor, Mich.: University Microfilm International, 1990.

Carew, Richard. *The Survey of Cornwall.* London: S.S., 1602; New York: Da Capo, 1969.

Carpenter, Brian. "Cricket in Teignmouth, 1773," *Devon and Cornwall Notes and Queries* 37, no. 7 (Spring 1995): 218-20.

Compact Guide: Cornwall. Rev. ed. Maspeth, N.Y.: Langenscheidt Publishers, 2000.

Copeland, Louis A. "The Cornish of Southwestern Wisconsin," *Collections of the State Historical Society of Wisconsin* 14 (1898): 301-34.

Cornish, Joseph E. *The History and Genealogy of Cornish Families in America.* Boston: George H. Ellis Company, 1987.

Crary, Rachel L. "Miss Cecil Grylls: Painter, Playwright, Adventurer," *Harlow's Wooden Man* 35, no. 4 (Fall 1999): 8-10.

Dorson, Richard M. *Bloodstoppers and Bearwalkers: Folk Traditions of the Upper Peninsula.* Cambridge, Mass.: Harvard University Press, 1952.

———. "Folk Traditions of the Upper Peninsula," *Michigan History* 31 (1947): 48-65.

Dudley, Terry. "Visiting Cornish Jacks in Mexico," *Cornish World* 2 (September–November 1994): 28.

Emerick, Lon L. *Going Back to Central: On the Road in Search of the Past in Michigan's Upper Peninsula.* Skandia, Mich.: North Country Publishing, 2003.

Ewart, Shirley, with Harold T. George. *Highly Respectable Families: The Cornish of Grass Valley, California, 1854-1954.* Grass Valley, Calif: Comstock Bonanza Press, 1998.

Fisher, Jane. "Michigan's Cornish People," *Michigan History* 29 (1945): 377-87.

Forster, John H. "Life in the Copper Mines of Lake Superior," *Michigan Pioneer and Historical Collection* 11 (1887): 175-86.

Frimodig, David Mac. "... With Mayt, Turmit, and Tatey," *Michigan Natural Resources Magazine* 40 (January–February 1971): 20-24.

Gates, William B., Jr. *Michigan Copper and Boston Dollars: An Economic History of the Copper Mining Industry.* Cambridge: Harvard University Press, 1954.

Graff, George P. *The People of Michigan.* Lansing: Michigan Department of Education, State Library Services, 1974.

Hatcher, Harlan. *A Century of Iron Men.* Indianapolis: Bobbs-Merrill, 1950.

History of the Upper Peninsula of Michigan. Chicago: Western Historical Company, 1883.

Hobart, Henry. *Copper Country Journal: The Diary of Schoolmaster Henry Hobart, 1863–1864*. Edited by Philip P. Mason. Detroit: Wayne State University Press, 1991.

"How Cornish Folk Fared in the Safe Hands of Uncle Sid," *Cornish World* 2 (September–November 1994): 6–7.

Jamison, James K. "The Copper Rush of the 50s," *Michigan History* 19 (1935): 371–90.

Jarve, Judith Rowe, ed. "From the Journal of Alfred Nicholls, Central Mine School Teacher and Principal, 1890–1925." In *Central Mine: Years of Hard Work—Lives of Pain and Hope*, compiled by Keweenaw County Historical Society. Eagle Harbor, Mich.: Keweenaw County Historical Society, 1998.

Jenkin, Alfred K. Hamilton. *Cornwall and Its People*. London, 1945; New York: A. M. Kelley, 1970.

Jopling, James E. "Cornish Miners of the Upper Peninsula," *Michigan History* 12 (July 1928): 554–67.

Keweenaw County Historical Society, comp. *Central Mine: Years of Hard Work—Lives of Pain and Hope*. Eagle Harbor, Mich.: Keweenaw County Historical Society, 1998.

"The Keweenaw Peninsula of Upper Michigan," *Cornish World* 4 (March–May 1995): 6–7.

Lankton, Larry. *Beyond the Boundaries: Life and Landscape at the Lake Superior Copper Mines, 1840–1875*. New York: Oxford University Press, 1997.

———. *Cradle to Grave: Life, Work, and Death at the Lake Superior Copper Mines*. New York: Oxford University Press, 1991.

Lewis, Helen F. *Southeastern Michigan Pioneer Families Especially Lenawee County and New York Origins*. Rhinebeck, N.Y.: Kinship, 1994.

Lockwood, William G., and Yvonne R. Lockwood. "The Cornish Pasty in Northern Michigan." In *Michigan Folklife Reader*, edited by C. Kurt Dewhurst and Yvonne Lockwood. East Lansing: Michigan State University Press, 1987.

Lowry, H. D. "The Cornish Cook," *Cornish World* 1 (June 1994): 28–29.

———. "The Cornish Pasty: Its History and Lore." In *A Sense of Place, Michigan's Upper Peninsula*, edited by Russell M. Magnaghi and Michael T. Marsden. Marquette: Northern Michigan University Press and The Center of Upper Peninsula Studies, 1997.

———. *A Preliminary History of the Order, Sons of St. George in Michigan*. Marquette, Mich.: Belle Fontaine Press, 2003.

Martin, John B. *Call It North Country: The Story of Upper Michigan*. New York: Alfred A. Knopf, 1944.

Marvin, John E. *History of Methodism in the Upper Peninsula of Michigan.* Detroit: Historical Society of Detroit, 1955.

Merrick, Hettie. *The Pasty.* Redruth, Cornwall: Tor Mark Press, 1995.

Monette, Clarence J. *Central Mine—A Ghost Town.* Calumet, Mich.: Greenlee Printing Company, 1995.

Murdoch, Angus. *Boom Copper: The Story of the First U.S. Mining Boom.* Calumet, Mich.: privately printed, 1943.

Nichols, Alfred. *More Copper Country Tales.* Calumet, Mich.: privately printed, 1968.

Pellowe, Susan. *Saffron & Currants: A Cornish Heritage Cookbook.* Rev. edition. Aurora, Ill.: Renard Productions, 1998.

Portrait and Biographical Album of Jackson County, Michigan. Chicago: Chapman Brothers, 1890.

Reports of the Immigration Commission. Immigrants in Industries. 41 vols. Washington, D.C.: Government Printing Office, 1911.

Robinson, Orrin W. *Early Days of the Lake Superior Copper Country.* Houghton, Mich.: privately printed, 1938.

Rowse, John. *The Hard Rock Men: Cornish Immigrants and the North American Mining Frontier.* New York: Barnes & Noble, 1974.

Rowse, A. L. *The Cousin Jacks: The Cornish in America.* New York: Charles Scribner's Sons, 1969.

Sawyer, Alvah L. *A History of the Northern Peninsula of Michigan and Its People.* 3 vols. Chicago: Lewis Publishing Company, 1911.

Stern, Jane, and Michael Stern. *Real American Food.* New York: Alfred Knopf, 1986.

Thomas, Newton G. *The Long Winter Ends.* New York: Macmillan, 1941; Detroit: Wayne State University Press, 1998.

Thurner, Arthur W. *Calumet Copper and People.* Chicago, Ill.: privately printed, 1974.

———. *Rebels on the Range: The Michigan Copper Miners Strike 1913–1914.* Lake Linden, Mich.: John H. Forster Press, 1984.

———. *Strangers and Sojourners: A History of Michigan's Keweenaw Peninsula.* Detroit: Wayne State University Press, 1994.

Todd, Arthur C. *The Cornish Miner in America.* Glendale, Calif.: Arthur Clark Company, 1967.

Vander Hill, C. Warren. *Settling the Great Lakes Frontier: Immigration of Michigan, 1837–1924.* Lansing: Michigan Historical Commission, 1970.

Vivian, C. H. "Cornwall's Legacy to American Mining," *Compressed Air Magazine* 75, no. 3 (March 1970): 6–8; 75, no. 4 (April 1970): 91–93; 75, no. 5 (May 1970): 7–9.

Voelker, John D. *Danny and the Boys: Being Some Legends of Hungry Hollow.* Cleveland and New York: World Publishing Company, 1951; Detroit: Wayne State University Press, 1987.

———. *Laughing Whitefish.* New York: McGraw-Hill Book Company, 1965.

———. *Trouble-Shooter: The Story of A Northwoods Prosecutor.* New York: Viking Press, 1943.

Whitaker, Joe Russell. *Negaunee, Michigan: An Urban Center Dominated by Iron Mining.* Chicago: University of Chicago Libraries, 1931.

Williams, Douglas. "Across the Atlantic in Search of Work," *Western Morning News,* 27 December 1995.

Index